Little Italy Cookbook

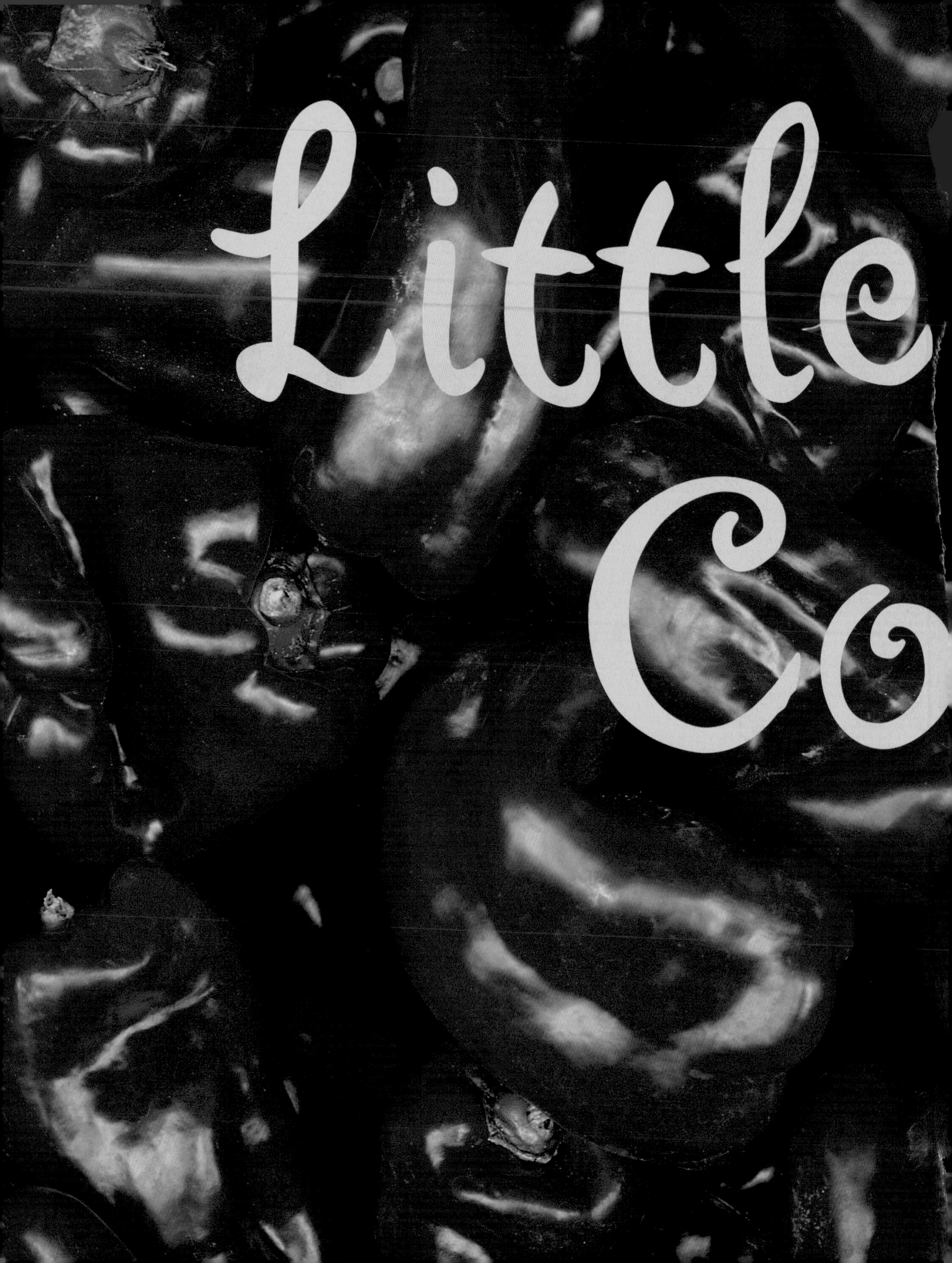
Little
Co

Italy okbook

David Ruggerio

Photographs by Melanie Acevedo

 ARTISAN · NEW YORK

Designer: Alexandra Maldonado
Production director: Hope Koturo

Library of Congress Cataloging-in-Publication Data
Ruggerio, David.
Little Italy Cookbook / David Ruggerio; photographs by
Melanie Acevedo
p.   cm..
Includes index.
ISBN 1–885183–54–2
1. Cookery, Italian. 2. Italian-Americans--New York
(State)--New york--Social life and customs.
3. Little Italy (New York, N.Y.)--Social life and customs.
I. Title.
TX723.R86 1997
641.5945--dc21   97-15261
CIP

Published in 1997 by Artisan,
a Division of Workman Publishing Company, Inc.
708 Broadway, New York, NY 10003

Printed in Italy
10 9 8 7 6 5 4 3 2

To Lisa,
I miss you every day

Table of

Introduction 8

Contents

La Caccia   120

La caccia, the hunt, always meant brisk days in the country, the companionship of close friends and family, and the great meals and story-telling that accompanied these special times. Whether we were hunting mushrooms for the sauce or game for the main dish, these hearty dishes—Polenta with Wild Mushrooms, Pumpkin Gnocchi, Rigatoni with Mushroom Sauce, Wild Duck with Lentils—always tasted just right when we came in from the cold.

La Festa   142

The two biggest and most sacred holidays in our culture are, of course, Christmas and Easter. Special seafood dishes, such as Christmas Eve Fried Eels, Christmas Fish Stew, and Baccala with Potatoes and Olives, always signaled Christmastime, while Easter celebrations called for the traditional Roasted Suckling Lamb, Pizza Rustica, and Pizza di Grano (Grain Pie).

Dolci   168

Like most people I know, I have a sweet tooth. Luckily for me, the cuisine of Little Italy features many excellent desserts, from simple Almond Biscotti to rich Zabaglione. This chapter also includes fruit-based delicacies such as Sicilian Citrus Granita, Honey-Fried Canteloupe, and Peaches in Red Wine, as well as the incomparable Amaretto-Chocolate Cheesecake.

Amici   194

Friends are sacred to Italian-Americans. The recipes in this chapter are adapted from dishes my friends have cooked for me over the years, including Cousin Vinny's Linguine with Scallop Sauce, Tortellini alla Danny, Mamma Palumbo's Egg Croquettes, and Joey "Bats'" Cannelloni.

Introduction

By profession, I am a gourmet chef. I trained in France and also in French kitchens in my native New York City. I am the chef-owner of several "fancy" restaurants in and around Manhattan, including Le Chantilly, Nonna, Maxim's, Chaz & Wilson's, and Pastis. So what's a guy with these credentials doing writing a book about Italian-American family cooking?

By birth, I am a typical Italian-American guy from Brooklyn. I grew up playing in the streets of neighborhoods like Bensonhurst, Flatbush, Canarsie, and Park Slope, where I lived. I also grew up in my grandmother's kitchen, asking a lot of questions. I boxed, and even had a successful two-year pro career. I worked as a bouncer at a disco in the late Seventies. And, like any self-respecting kid from Brooklyn, I fooled around some and got into a little trouble. But for as long as I can remember, I always wanted to be a chef. I was lucky because my roots were in the Italian-American culture, where love of food is so important.

In the time and place that I grew up, though, there weren't really any great Italian restaurants. They were mostly mom-and-pop operations, serving bastardized Neapolitan cooking. I began my "culinary career" in a neighborhood Italian restaurant in Sheepshead Bay called the Grotta D'Oro. I was 14 years old and I was working there five or six days a week, nights, and after school. I washed dishes, chopped vegetables, peeled garlic, did all the basic kitchen work. It was a good experience, but eventually I realized if I wanted to make it as a chef I would have to move on.

At about the same time I started to get into boxing. My uncle Eddie Gavin first got me involved in the sport. He was a top-notch fighter and three-time Golden Gloves champ who turned professional. Eddie had started his sons, my cousins, boxing, and I used to watch them fight. I told my **uncle** I wanted to fight, too, so he set me up at Izzy Zerling's gym. I fought 98 amateur fights, then decided to go professional. I fought 17 pro fights and did quite well. I won the first 10 with 10 knockouts; I was featured on Len Berman's "Sports Spectacular," and a few other local shows; I even went up to Brockton, Massachusetts, and sparred with Marvin Hagler.

Meanwhile, I was still intent on becoming a chef. One of the hottest **French** restaurants in New York at the time was La Caravelle. I worked at a few other places first, including Tavern on the Green, to get my feet wet. Then I started going to La Caravelle and asking for a job. They'd tell me to come back in one or two months. I must have gone there 13 times before they gave me a **job**. I guess they figured out if they didn't I was never going to leave them alone.

La Caravelle was difficult at first. It was an old-style French kitchen, very disciplined. All the commands were in French. This Italian kid from **Brooklyn** didn't speak any French, but I learned fast. After a year of working there and hearing that if you didn't work in France you were nothing, I decided to go to France.

It was 1982 and I was lucky enough to land a spot at the Hotel Negresco in Nice (two Michelin stars) under chef Jacques Maximin. After a year, I returned to **La Caravelle**, continued to work my way up the ranks until, in 1988, I was promoted to chef de cuisine. After a total of nine years at La Caravelle, I was hired by the Pierre Cardin organization to head the kitchen at the

New York branch of Maxim's, where I received three stars from the *New York Times*. After Cardin closed Maxim's in 1992, I moved a few blocks down and across on 57th Street to take over the kitchen at Le Chantilly. From there, I've branched out as executive chef at a number of other restaurants, but I'm getting away from my story. . . .

Toward the end of my boxing career, in the mid-1980s, when I had already trained in France and been promoted to sous-chef at La Caravelle, I would come in on Monday mornings all banged up from my weekends in the ring. A lot of the fights took place on Saturday nights and as a sous-chef you can't keep asking for Saturday nights off. It became obvious that I was going to have to give up either cooking or boxing. It was a very tough choice. Boxing is the most exciting thing I can imagine, but I finally decided to dedicate myself to cooking.

Since those days, with some luck and some hard work, I've met with a good measure of success as a gourmet chef, and I'm still working hard to earn more. But I've never lost touch with my roots, with the great immigrant tradition of my parents, their parents, their parents' parents. In some ways, I'm living in two worlds: the streets of Little Italy and the world of nouvelle haute cuisine. Sometimes the two worlds meet in an ingredient, in a recipe, in an influence. Sometimes I marry the two consciously in a dish for one of my restaurants; other times, I do it unconsciously.

Like many cooking professionals, I have a very large cookbook collection. I've wanted to write a cookbook for some time now, to share my love of cooking with fellow food lovers and cookbook aficionados. There's a good chance I'll write a gourmet cookbook someday, but when I started thinking about writing this book, the only plan that really made sense was to return to my Italian roots, to the cooking that comes from my heart, not from my head.

It's not hard for me to go back to my **roots** in Brooklyn, because that's what I do all the time. I stay in touch with friends and family: people like my cousin Danny who helps run a vegetable wholesaler; my grandmother who lives in the suburbs of Long Island but still cooks Italian for me every **weekend**; my Uncle Frankie, who has the lobster dock on Flatbush Avenue; my friend Joe, who has the bread store; and the old man Carmine, who still picks the mushrooms.

This is not a book about Italian cooking; it is a book about **Italian-American** cooking. Many of the foods or the dishes in this book didn't even exist back in Italy, but every one bears the stamp of the Italian immigrant experience. This is the food I call Italian Soul Food.

In putting this book together, I spent a lot of time talking to my relatives and friends about Italian-American food. Several key elements came up again and again. **Frugality** may be the most important principle. The first Italian immigrants were poor people from Southern Italy and Sicily who came to America looking for a better life. The immigrant experience was all about making do with what you had, relying heavily on your ingenuity and resourcefulness.

The Italian immigrants were the first vegetarians in the United States—not because they wanted to be, but because they didn't have a choice. To most Italians, even in Italy, meat is not something you eat every day. It's reserved for special occasions, **holidays**, for a feast. Today, that hard-and-fast frugality is still practiced by the older people, even if they've become prosperous and moved out of the old neighborhoods. They still work wonders with just a little bit of rice, potato, or **pasta**, some garlic, onions, and tomatoes. In my family, even when we were living comfortably, we would save all the left-overs in recycled ricotta cheese containers. Not even a paper bag was thrown away.

Another element of Italian-American cooking is improvisation. You start with a recipe, often related by word of mouth, that has simple **ingredients** and basic procedures. You go home and execute it your own way. I can give a recipe to ten different people and they can follow it ten different ways and it comes out great each way. So it's not necessarily about following a recipe exactly, but about how much of yourself you put into that recipe.

The best cooks I've seen, even if they aren't Italian, become Italian when they cook Italian **food**. (Keep in mind when I say "Italian," I really mean "Italian-American." Also, remember that "Italian" is short for "Italian-American food," as in the famous statement "I eat Italian seven days a week.") They put on the **music**,

they have a glass of wine. They play the part. Their grandmother might as well be from Calabria or Sicily, at least for a couple hours. Believe it or not, having the correct **mindset** adds to the cooking. Otherwise, it's just a little bit of olive oil, a little bit of garlic, a little bit of basil. So what? It becomes so much more than that because of the **pride**, the love, and the passion that Italian-Americans have for their culture and their food. I know there are other cultures that cook with the same pride and **care**, but I can only speak first-hand about the Italian-Americans.

Of all the people who inspired this book, my grandmother, my **nonna**, Mary Lazzarino, is by far Number One. She is the center of the family and her day revolves around cooking. For my grandmother, planning the family dinner starts each morning, sometimes as much as two or three days earlier. There aren't any last-minute decisions. When I was growing up, I would never come home and find just a piece of meat on the table. It was always a multicourse meal. And if it wasn't a multicourse meal at home, it was out to dinner at restaurants, which is another reason why, from a young age, I had this ambition to become a chef.

I have written this book for all those people who had great-grandparents or grandparents or aunts who cooked Italian-American food for them when they were young. They may have distant memories of these dishes but the recipes are long gone. This book is a way to not only recreate those dishes, but also recapture memories of the whole family sitting around the table, the nephews, the nieces, the cousins, thirty people at the table. . . .

I also wrote this book for those who were not fortunate enough to be born Italian or who never had any contact with Italian culture. We'll go back to the old neighborhoods and the family gatherings and see what the second and third generations are cooking at home. In addition to the beautiful recipes that have been handed down to me, from my grandmother, from my friends in Little Italy, I also want you to meet the people, soak up the lore, and experience the love that goes into making this simple, frugal cuisine great.

The chapters of the book celebrate the people, places, and events that form the basis of my Italian heritage. I begin, of course, with Nonna's recipes, then head to Mulberry Street, then on to Sheepshead Bay for seafood, and to Mimmo's Garden for recipes of the harvest. Then come two chapters for special times of the year: La Caccia presents the hearty dishes of the hunting season, and La Festa offers all the special dishes of the holidays and feast days that are so dear to the hearts of all Italians. Finally, we finish with Dolci (my favorite part of a meal) and some of the best recipes from my Amici, my friends.

onna

The Italian word for grandmother evokes special memories of childhood. It is the *nonna* who

epitomizes the warmth of the **home** and all the love that goes into Italian-American

cooking. In this chapter you will find the special recipes that my grandmother cooked for me. It's

the next best thing to having her in your kitchen.

My *nonna*, Mary Lazzarino, is 80 years young. She is my mother's mother and they come

from Sant' Angela di Lombardi, a short distance outside of Naples. My mother died when I was

young so my **grandmother** raised me. She also raised my cousins, and she's helped

raise my kids, the third generation. She's the patriarch and matriarch all rolled into one. A very

strong person. I go out to Long Island to see her every weekend. She does the cooking, just like

always. She has her own ways in the kitchen and I don't interfere, even if I am an *Executive Chef*. What she does in the kitchen may look simple, but it took a lifetime of experience to learn. Much of her day, probably 80 or 90 percent, is centered around food, be it preserving vegetables, baking bread or cookies, cooking the gravy, or tending the garden. She is very particular about everything, from what pan she likes to use to sauté peppers to which store she likes to buy a certain type of olive oil from. She makes poor Vito the butcher show her eight different pieces of meat before she chooses the one she wants. She goes to one particular market because they play Jerry Vale music. She learned to cook from her mother, who learned to cook from *her* mother, and so on and so forth.

Like most older Italian women, Nonna has a partner in crime. Hers is Aunt Angie. Angie is my grandmother's aunt—her mother's sister—but she is actually two years younger than Nonna. Aunt Angie is in her late seventies

and still swears that her fire-engine red hair is her own. The two of them devote their

lives to family, food, Atlantic City on Thursdays, and of course confession at church on

Fridays. Now for Italians, especially the women, "coonfession" is one of the high-

lights of the week, not to be missed. I remember one eventful Friday Angie didn't feel well and

told my grandmother she couldn't go to church. Nonna, fear-

ing for Angie's eternal soul, told her to tell her her sins and she

would relay them to the priest. The next day my grandmother

was in a very bad mood. We asked what was the matter and

she exclaimed, "That Angie, she's a swinger. She never told me

all that stuff before!" So much for second-hand confessions.

I remember Nonna and my aunts would always go food

shopping together in a group. They turned it into

an art form. We used to live on Berkeley Place in the Park

Slope section of Brooklyn. In those days, the neighborhood was predominantly Italian and

Orthodox Jewish. Of course, each of these groups had their # traditions and

superstitions, which would come into play when the women went shopping. The Italian women figured out that the Jewish shopkeepers had a superstition: If they didn't make a sale to the first person who walked into their store in the morning, it meant bad luck for the rest of the day. So Nonna and the aunts would make a point of being the first ones in the store. Then they would haggle over the price. The Orthodox Jews were smart; they learned to speak Italian better than some of the Italians who came to their stores. But the Italian women knew they had an advantage. If they didn't get what they wanted at the price they wanted, they'd turn around

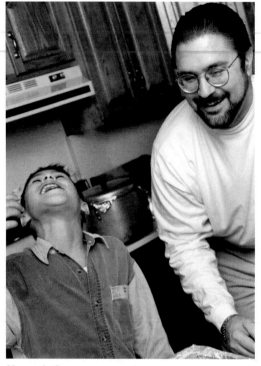

My son Anthony

and walk out. They might walk out of a store two or three times before they were satisfied with the price they got. The merchants would chase them out of the store, pull them back in, and haggle some more until they finally made the sale.

There were live kosher chicken markets in Park Slope. Some of them are still there. There were rabbits, too. Nonna would never buy just any old store-bought chicken when she could have a fresh kosher one. For the holidays, you could buy a live lamb in those markets. They would either slaughter it for you on the spot, or you could take it home live. The shopkeepers didn't care; they were just happy to make a sale.

While I'm on the subject of my grandmother, I should also mention her husband Leonard, my grandfather. He died when I was about 12 years old, but in the short time I knew him, he had a tremendous impact on my life. He was a man of great integrity, honor, and pride—all the qualities you expect in an Italian. His father was an orphan, the result of a midnight rendezvous between a local girl and the monsignor of the church. His father was adopted

My son Paul

by a family named Lazzarino, who raised him. Later he married and had five children. The youngest was my grandfather. When Leonard was 11 years old, his father was killed by his stepbrother in an argument. Leonard had a hard life as a kid, but he went on to educate himself, and rose to become the head of the Department of Corrections in New York City. My grandfather had three great loves in his life: my grandmother, food, and storytelling. I share these same loves, and have tried to bring them all together in this chapter.

Zuppa di Pane

BREAD SOUP

Italian-Americans are known for their resourcefulness in the kitchen, and my grandmother is no exception. She never wastes anything, including the leftover bread. This hearty recipe is a prime example of that resourcefulness.

In my family, we like to puree only half the beans and leave the rest whole. Note that you'll have to soak the beans overnight and that you'll probably want to puree them in a food processor, unless you want to use an old-fashioned food mill, which is a little more difficult, but definitely more authentic and interesting. This recipe also works well with split peas.

Serves 6 as a first course or 4 as a main dish

1 pound dried cannellini beans

3 quarts water

1½ teaspoons salt

½ teaspoon pepper

¼ cup plus 3 tablespoons olive oil

2 bunches Swiss chard (or spinach leaves)

1 large onion, chopped

3 carrots, diced small

2 celery stalks, diced small

1 tablespoon tomato paste

1 loaf stale Italian bread, cut into ½-inch slices

1 tablespoon chopped fresh Italian parsley

1 tablespoon chopped fresh basil

Soak the beans overnight in a large bowl with enough water to cover by 2 inches. Drain the beans and run them under cool water. Place the drained beans in a large pot with the 3 quarts of water over high heat. Add the salt, ¼ teaspoon of the pepper, and the 3 tablespoons of olive oil to the water; bring to a boil then lower the heat and cook the beans about 1 hour or until tender. Remove a third of the beans and reserve for garnish; leave the remaining beans in their cooking water.

Remove the stems of the Swiss chard and finely julienne. Reserve the leaves. Add the Swiss chard stems, onion, carrots, celery, tomato paste, and the remaining ¼ teaspoon pepper to the cooked beans. Bring to a boil and cover. Reduce the heat to medium-low and cook for about 1 hour or until the vegetables and beans are very tender.

Meanwhile, preheat the oven to 375° F. Slice the Italian bread and brush it with the remaining ¼ cup olive oil. Place on a baking sheet and toast in the oven until golden brown.

Remove the center rib from the reserved Swiss chard leaves and cut each leaf into eighths.

When the soup is ready, ladle the hot mixture into a blender and puree. (It should have a thick winter-soup consistency; if too thick, add some boiling water.) Mix in the parsley, basil, reserved beans, and cut-up Swiss chard leaves. Adjust the seasoning to taste.

Place 2 slices of toasted bread in each serving bowl, ladle the soup on top and serve immediately.

The Perfect Crust

When you're baking bread, to assure a nice, crisp crust, place a metal pan in the bottom of the oven. As soon as you put the bread in the oven, throw a handful of ice into the pan. Repeat this process two or three times during baking. The steam created when the ice melts and evaporates in the oven gives the bread a light, crispy coating with just the right sheen. Commercial ovens have an automatic valve that periodically injects steam during baking. The ice-in-the-pan trick is your home remedy; without it, you are going to get bread with a dull, soft crust.

Ciabatta

SANDWICH ROLLS

These rolls are the basis for my grandmother's delicious sandwiches—*panini*. She fills them with a variety of meats and other fillings—prosciutto, salami, cheese, or just peppers and scrambled eggs. We used to snack on Nonna's *panini* almost every day when we came home from school. You will find this dough is wetter than any other bread dough and easiest to prepare in a mixer with a dough hook. But don't worry, you'll end up with a crust that is incredibly crisp and thin, and bread that is the tenderest you will ever taste.

Makes 12 small loaves

Starter
1¹/₂ teaspoons dry yeast
1 cup lukewarm water
1¹/₂ cups sifted bread flour

Dough
1¹/₂ teaspoons dry yeast
¹/₂ cup lukewarm water
2 cups ice water
1 cup starter
6 cups sifted bread flour
1 tablespoon salt
olive oil for brushing
cornmeal for baking
ice cubes for baking

To make the starter: Dissolve the yeast in the warm water. Add the flour and stir until well-blended. The mixture should have the consistency of a thick batter. Pour the mixture into a lightly oiled bowl and cover with plastic wrap. Allow to rise for 3 hours until tripled in volume. Reserve.

To make the dough: Dissolve the yeast in the lukewarm water and let stand for 10 minutes. In a mixer, combine the yeast mixture, ice water, starter, flour, and salt. Mix at medium speed with the paddle attachment for 3 minutes. The dough will look soupy. Let the dough rest for 20 minutes. After the rest period, start to knead the dough in the mixer with the dough hook for 15 to 20 minutes. If you don't have a mixer with a dough hook, use a food processor with a plastic dough blade or do it the old-fashioned way—with your hands. (*Note*: The dough should stay at room temperature and should not feel warm to the touch. As you mix it, if it starts to overheat, stop and allow it to cool.) After 20 minutes, the dough should pull away completely from the sides and bottom of the bowl. At this point, reduce the speed and knead until the dough is smooth and satiny, about 6 to 7 minutes.

Transfer the dough to a large, lightly oiled baking pan. Lightly brush the top of the dough with oil. Cover with plastic wrap and allow to rise until tripled in volume, about 2½ hours. (The ideal temperature for the rising is 74° F.) Once it has risen, pour the dough onto a well-floured surface and shape the loaves. Use about ¼ cup of dough for each loaf. Set the loaves in a cool spot, dust with flour, then cover with plastic wrap and allow to rise again until doubled in size, about 2 hours.

Place an unglazed ceramic tile or baking stone on the oven's lowest rack and preheat the oven to 450° F. Just before putting the bread in the oven, sprinkle the stone with cornmeal to prevent the loaves from sticking. Place the loaves on the stone and place a metal pan of ice cubes on the bottom of the oven to produce steam. Bake until dark brown, about 30 minutes. Allow to cool on a rack for 1 hour before eating.

These delectable little rolls should be eaten fresh the day they're made. The leftovers—if there are any—can be toasted and added to a soup or used as the main ingredient for bread salad *(panzanella)*.

Minestra Maritata

SICILIAN VEGETABLE SOUP

This hearty soup, which comes from Sicily, can easily be a full meal as well as a first course. *Maritata* is Sicilian slang for "married." The term applies to this soup since it marries such wonderful and diverse flavors.

Serves 6 as a first course or 4 as a main dish

1 piece prosciutto knuckle or bone

1 piece prosciutto rind, about 2 x 2 inches

9 cups chicken stock (see Basic Recipes, page 216)

¾ pound boneless pork shoulder, cut into ½-inch cubes and trimmed of all fat

6 ounces salami, cut into ¼-inch dice

2-inch piece Parmesan rind, cubed

⅛ teaspoon crushed red pepper flakes

1 onion, chopped

1 carrot, peeled and chopped

1 celery stalk, chopped

¾ pound savoy cabbage

¾ pound broccoli rabe

¾ pound escarole

grated Parmesan cheese, for garnish

Blanch the prosciutto bone and rind in boiling water for 5 minutes. Remove the bone and discard the water. Scrape any excess fat from the rind with a sharp knife, then cut rind into narrow strips.

Place the stock in a large pot and bring it to a boil. Add the prosciutto rind and bone, pork shoulder, salami, cheese rind, pepper flakes, onion, carrot, and celery. Let the liquid come to a boil again. Reduce the heat and allow to simmer for 1 hour.

Wash all the greens well. Discard the outer leaves of the cabbage and remove the core. Peel the stems of the broccoli rabe. Remove the center of the escarole leaves and discard. Chop all the greens and reserve.

When the soup has cooked for 1 hour, add the reserved greens and cook for another 30 minutes. Remove the prosciutto bone and rind and the cheese rind.

Ladle the soup into bowls, sprinkle with grated Parmesan and serve.

Bracciole

TRADITIONAL BRAISED BEEF

My father had a dog named Val after Rudolph Valentino. Val was very fond of my grandmother's *bracciole*. One day she was browning five *bracciole* in the frying pan and went out to hang some clothing on the line. When she came back, she only had three. Actually, Val loved all kinds of Italian food, not just the *bracciole*. He was the only dog I ever saw who ate macaroni.

You will need some wax paper to pound the meat thin and also some kitchen string to tie up the rolled *bracciole*. Serve this dish accompanied by pasta or potatoes.

Serves 4 as a main course

8 thin slices bottom round beef

3 tablespoons olive oil

¼ pound butter, melted

salt and pepper to taste

4 cloves garlic, chopped

3 tablespoons grated Parmesan cheese

1 cup breadcrumbs

½ cup chopped fresh Italian parsley

4 hard-boiled eggs, chopped

**1 recipe Garden Tomato Sauce
   (see Basic Recipes, page 217)**

Place the beef between two pieces of wax paper. Pound carefully with a meat pounder or a rolling pin until very thin. Remove the paper and rub the slices of meat with 2 tablespoons of the olive oil and all of the butter. Season with salt and pepper.

Make the filling by combining the garlic, cheese, breadcrumbs, parsley, and boiled eggs. Place equal portions of the mixture on each of the beef slices. Roll each slice up lengthwise so that it's long and narrow like a cigar then tie it together with kitchen string.

Heat the remaining 1 tablespoon of olive oil in a large pan over medium heat and lightly brown the meat rolls. Cover with the tomato sauce and simmer gently over low heat for 2 hours. Transfer to warm plates, spoon the tomato sauce on top and serve immediately alongside your favorite pasta.

Eggs in Purgatory

This was a traditional breakfast at the neighborhood luncheonette for all the guys after a long night out. The only problem was that Frankie the cook never made it as good or as spicy as my grandmother does.

Use a loaf of Italian bread that is about $4\frac{1}{2}$ inches in diameter so the slices will be big enough for an egg to fit inside the cored-out pieces.

Serves 4

Sauce

2 tablespoons olive oil

$\frac{1}{2}$ onion, finely chopped

1 teaspoon crushed red pepper flakes

3 cups diced, seeded, peeled tomatoes

2 tablespoons finely chopped fresh basil

2 tablespoons finely chopped fresh Italian parsley

4 $\frac{1}{2}$-inch-thick slices Italian bread

3 tablespoons olive oil

4 eggs

$\frac{1}{4}$ cup grated Parmesan cheese

To make the sauce: Heat the olive oil in a medium-size sauce pot over medium heat. Add the onion and cook for about 3 to 4 minutes or until it turns translucent. Add the red pepper flakes, tomatoes, basil, and parsley. Cook for about 20 minutes over low heat. Reserve.

Cut a circle in the center of each bread slice with a medium-size cookie cutter. Discard the cut centers. (You can give them to your kids or, if you don't have any, to the neighbors' kids; they love the soft insides of the bread.)

Heat the 3 tablespoons of olive oil in a large non-stick sauté pan. Place the bread slices in the oil. Cook on one side until nicely browned. Flip the slices onto the other side. Crack an egg into the center of each slice of bread. Continue to cook for about 3 to 4 minutes over medium heat until the eggs are firm. Carefully remove the bread-and-egg combination with a spatula and place on a plate. Top with the sauce, sprinkle with the cheese, and serve.

Escarole Soup with Meatballs

My grandmother still makes this delicious soup at least once a month. Her twist on the recipe is to add the egg and Parmesan cheese at the end—like a *stracciatella*, the classic Roman soup that is finished with a raw egg. She insists on using half beef, half veal, but I think this version with all-beef meatballs works equally well. (Sorry again, Nonna.) The meatballs from this recipe can also be used in a tomato sauce for pasta.

This recipe calls for pastina. Many of us have fond childhood memories of these tiny little pieces of pasta—when we were sick our mothers would make some with a little bit of cheese and butter. I'm an adult and I still love to eat pastina. It's Italian comfort food—great in just about any kind of soup. Pastina takes very little time to cook, and works well served with a little olive oil, a little butter, and a little Parmesan. You can feed it to children of any age, from infants to 80 year-olds.

Serves 6 as a first course

Meatballs

1/4 **pound ground beef**

1 **tablespoon grated Parmesan cheese**

1/2 **slice white bread, soaked in milk and squeezed dry**

1 **egg yolk**

1/4 **teaspoon salt**

1/8 **teaspoon white pepper**

1 **teaspoon chopped fresh Italian parsley**

Soup

4 **cups chicken stock (see Basic Recipes, page 216)**

1 **head escarole, washed and cut into 1/2-inch pieces**

1 **small onion, chopped**

3/4 **cup pastina**

2 **eggs**

1/8 **teaspoon salt**

2 **tablespoons grated Parmesan cheese**

To make the meatballs: Mix all the ingredients in a bowl. Take one tablespoon at a time and form into balls about 1 inch in diameter. Refrigerate the meatballs until you are ready to add them to the soup.

To make the soup: In a soup pot over medium heat, bring the chicken broth to a boil. Add the escarole, onion, and meatballs and cook for 3 minutes. Add the pastina and cook for an additional 4 to 5 minutes. In a bowl, whisk together the eggs, salt, and cheese. Reduce the heat on the soup and quickly whisk in the egg mixture. Allow to cook for 2 minutes, ladle into bowls, and serve immediately.

Brisket of Beef with Genoese Sauce

Here is a good example of Italian-American frugality and creativity, a hearty home-style recipe that I associate with my grandmother. One recipe like this can become two or three meals—it's good as a leftover and then again in a sandwich. Brisket is a lean cut of beef from the breast, a pot roast. It needs to be braised—cooked long and slow in liquid—so it doesn't dry out.

This recipe uses the liquid from the pot twice: first for a vinaigrette sauce to spoon over the meat, and second as a puree for the pasta. With a vegetable or salad on the side, this makes a big, hearty meal any time of year, but especially during the colder months.

Serves 4 as a main course

Brisket

4-pound brisket of beef

salt and pepper

3 tablespoons olive oil

4¹/₂ cups chicken stock, plus more as needed (see Basic Recipes, page 216)

3 pounds onions, sliced

¹/₂ pound carrots, sliced on a bias

¹/₄ pound salami, sliced to ¹/₄-inch julienne

¹/₄ pound prosciutto, sliced to ¹/₄-inch julienne

Vinaigrette

1 cup warm broth from the pot

5 tablespoons red wine vinegar

1 tablespoon finely chopped garlic

3 tablespoons olive oil

1 onion, chopped

¹/₂ cup chopped fresh Italian parsley

1 teaspoon salt

¹/₂ teaspoon white pepper

Pasta and Sauce

the remaining broth from the pot

salt and pepper to taste

¹/₂ pound fusilli, cooked

¹/₂ cup julienned fresh basil

To prepare the brisket: Preheat the oven to 375° F. Season the meat with salt and pepper. Heat the olive oil in a large pot over medium heat. (The pot should be just big enough to accommodate the meat; if it's too big, you'll need too much liquid in it.) Add the brisket and brown all over. Remove it from the pot and put it aside. Carefully drain the oil from the pot.

Add ¹/₂ cup of the chicken stock to the pot and return the pot to burner. Deglaze the pot by scraping the scraps from the browned meat with a wooden spoon until they are totally dislodged from the bottom. Add the onions, carrots, salami, and prosciutto, then the brisket. Add the remaining 4 cups of chicken stock or just enough to cover the meat about halfway. Bring the stock to a boil, then cover the pot and place in the oven for 3 hours.

Little Ears

Much like sun-dried tomatoes and broccoli rabe, orecchiette ("little ears") are a staple of Italian-American cooking that have become *très chic* in recent times. Most of the top *nouvelle* American chefs have had them on their menus. People have even learned to pronounce the word, which can be a tongue twister when you first encounter it.

I suspect orecchiette have become so popular because they're easy to eat. You can easily scoop up these solid chunks of pasta with a generous dollop of sauce in a spoon. With many other traditional pasta shapes, it's more complicated. For example, you have to wind linguine or spaghetti around your fork, and there's always the danger you'll splatter the front of your shirt. Orecchiette can be served as first or main courses.

Check every once in a while to make sure that the liquid hasn't evaporated; if the pot starts to get dry, add another cup of chicken stock. To check if meat is done, stick a fork in it; you should be able to remove the fork without resistance. Once the meat has cooked, skim any fat from the surface of the liquid. Leave the meat on the stove in the covered pot with no heat under it while you're making the vinaigrette.

To make the vinaigrette: Ladle out 1 cup of the brisket liquid into a bowl with the vinegar and garlic. (Reserve the rest of the contents of the pot.) Slowly whisk in the olive oil. Add the onion and parsley, then season with the salt and pepper.

When ready to serve, remove the meat from the pot, slice, and place on a warm serving platter. Spoon the vinaigrette over the sliced meat.

To make the pasta and sauce: Puree the remaining contents of the pot in a blender. Season with salt and pepper and serve on the side of the meat with the cooked fusilli, sprinkling the basil on top.

Orecchiette with Peas and Prosciutto

This recipe is very easy and is truly one of my favorites. I have fond memories of my sister Lisa helping my grandmother make this dish from scratch, including the macaroni. Lisa would push her thumb into the small balls of pasta dough to form the "little ears."

You can buy orecchiette fresh, frozen, or dry. If you can't find fresh peas for this recipe, use frozen instead of canned. Frozen peas are the next best thing to fresh.

My grandmother would serve such a dish as the first course for a large meal and maybe as the main dish for lunch. You can also serve it as a main course for dinner, if you like.

Serves 6 as a first course or 4 as a main dish

1 pound orecchiette

¹/₂ cup olive oil

¹/₂ pound prosciutto, diced

1 tablespoon finely chopped onion

¹/₂ teaspoon crushed red pepper flakes

1¹/₂ cups peas, cooked

2 tablespoons butter

¹/₂ cup grated Parmesan cheese

Cook the pasta according to the instructions on the package.

Heat the olive oil in a large sauté pan over medium heat. Add the prosciutto and cook until nicely browned. Add the onion and sauté for another 2 minutes. Add the pepper flakes and peas and cook for 1 minute more. Remove from the heat. Toss in the cooked pasta, then the butter and cheese. Spoon into bowls or dishes and serve immediately.

Prosciutto Bread

This recipe comes from my great grandmother, Antoinette, who was Nonna's mother. She used to cook with "leaf lard," which is rendered pork fat. She would buy 50 pounds of the stuff at a time at Benny's Pork Store in Brooklyn. She was such a strong woman, she would carry that 50-pound vat home herself. When she rendered the fat, the result was cracklings. She would make a bread with the cracklings, some diced prosciutto, salami, and whatever other meats were around. I've taken the rendered pork fat out of this version, figuring not too many people follow that procedure anymore. Otherwise, this is her recipe.

Serves 6 as a side dish or snack

2 envelopes dry yeast

1½ cups warm water

3½ cups all-purpose flour

1 teaspoon salt

1 teaspoon black peppercorns, coarsely cracked

1 teaspoon garlic, finely chopped

6 ounces prosciutto, diced very small

6 ounces Genoa salami, diced very small

⅓ cup olive oil

1 cup provolone cheese, chopped well

1 egg

ice cubes for baking

Preheat the oven to 400° F.

Dissolve the yeast in the warm water. Place the flour and yeast in a mixer with a dough hook attachment. Add the salt and pepper. Mix at medium speed for about 7 minutes. Add the garlic, meats, oil, and cheese. Let the machine work it for another 3 minutes.

Line a baking pan with parchment paper. Divide the mixture in two. Form the two halves into round balls and place on the prepared pan. Cover the dough with a damp towel and leave in a warm area for about ½ hour or until the dough doubles in size.

With a sharp knife, score the dough balls: make slits about ½-inch long in a criss-cross pattern—or whatever other pattern you like—making sure the slits cut through the crust to act as steam vents during the baking process. Beat the egg and brush generously over the top and sides of the dough—don't let it drip onto the paper. Bake for 25 to 30 minutes or until you can insert a toothpick in it

and the toothpick comes out clean. Remove from the oven and allow to cool. Cut the loaves into thick slices or wedges and serve.

The prosciutto bread is best eaten right away, but you can refrigerate it for a day or two. You can also wrap the bread in plastic wrap and freeze it for up to a month.

Frittata Contadina

FARM-STYLE OMELET

A frittata is an Italian-style open omelet. For this farm-style frittata, any little mushroom, pepper, or potato will make a wonderful addition. Frittata can be eaten for breakfast, lunch, or dinner, or cold as a late-night snack. You can even put it between two pieces of bread to make a sandwich. My grandmother likes to dice up the leftover frittata and put it in the next day's salad.

Serves 4

¼ cup olive oil

1 small onion, thinly sliced

8 eggs

¼ pound mozzarella cheese, finely shredded

1 tablespoon chopped fresh basil

salt to taste

Preheat the oven to 350° F.

Heat the olive oil in a nonstick sauté pan over medium heat. Add the onion and cook until translucent, about 3 minutes.

While the onion is cooking, place the eggs in a bowl and beat with a fork. Add the salt and mix in the cheese and basil. Pour the mixture onto the onions in the pan.

Cook for about 1 minute then place in the oven for 5 to 10 minutes or until firm in the center. Carefully flip onto a plate and serve.

Leftovers may be stored for a couple of days in the fridge.

Polenta Pizzas

Here is a dish that's great for kids—it's a little different from regular pizza, but it's called pizza nonetheless. I loved it when my grandmother made them for me and now she makes them for my sons Anthony and Paul, who love them too. I've called for regular yellow cornmeal in this recipe to make the polenta in about 30 minutes. But it can be just as successful—and I know this statement is going to upset a lot of traditionalists —if you use the quick-cooking polenta mixes. They are just as good and save time and trouble.

Serves 8 or makes about 16 pizzas

5 ounces pancetta, finely minced

4 cups water

1 tablespoon salt

1 cup coarse yellow cornmeal

½ cup shredded mozzarella cheese

½ cup shredded fontina cheese

½ cup grated Parmesan cheese

¼ cup julienned fresh basil

Preheat the oven to 450° F.

Cook the pancetta in a skillet over low heat until slightly crisp. Reserve along with the drippings.

Bring the water to a boil in a deep saucepan over medium heat. Add the salt and cornmeal. Cook stirring frequently, until the mixture is thick and pulls away from the side of the pan, about 30 minutes. Stir in the pancetta and the drippings. Immediately pour into an oiled 11 x 17-inch baking pan, spreading evenly. Allow to cool. When firm, cut as many 3-inch rounds as possible using a cookie cutter, a knife, or an upside-down coffee cup pressed down. Place the rounds on a cookie sheet. Combine the cheeses and basil and sprinkle generously on top of each round. Bake until the cheese melts and the polenta is brown and crispy, about 7 to 8 minutes. Serve immediately as part of an antipasto, as a snack, or as a full meal for kids.

Parmesan Mashed Potatoes

Here's an Italian-American variation on every kid's favorite all-American dish, mashed potatoes. It goes well with meat or poultry. It's also an excellent substitute for polenta, or served as a snack by itself with just a piece of crusty Italian bread. My grandmother likes to serve it with pot roast (see Brisket of Beef with Genoese Sauce, page 27).

Serves 4 as a side dish

3 large Idaho potatoes, peeled
3 tablespoons butter
$^1/_2$ cup grated Parmesan cheese
1 cup milk, warmed
salt and white pepper to taste

Place the potatoes in a pot of salted water. Bring to a boil and cook until tender. Drain and pass the potatoes through a food mill into a bowl. (If you don't have a food mill, mash them by hand. For those of you who are lazy and feel inclined to use a food processor, I have one word of advice: *don't*—you're likely to end up with an overly starchy mess.) Transfer back to the pot and stir in the butter, cheese, and milk over low heat. Season with salt and pepper and serve piping hot.

Sweet and Sour Peppers

My grandmother always includes this dish as part of the antipasto plate. It's also great served at room temperature as a side dish with some cold leftover pork or veal. My father swears the dish is Sicilian because of the raisins. But then my father always swears anything good is Sicilian.

Serves 4 as an appetizer or side dish

3 red peppers
3 green peppers
3 tablespoons olive oil
$^1/_3$ cup slivered almonds
$^1/_3$ cup raisins, soaked in water and drained
$^1/_4$ cup chicken stock
2 tablespoons sugar
$^1/_4$ cup red wine vinegar
$^3/_4$ teaspoon salt

Peel the skin off the peppers with a vegetable peeler. Core and remove the seeds. Slice the peppers into $^1/_2$-inch strips. Heat the olive oil in a sauté pan over medium heat. Add the pepper strips and sauté for about 4 minutes. Add the remaining ingredients and continue to cook for 15 minutes. Remove from the heat and allow to cool to room temperature before serving. This dish may be stored in the refrigerator for up to one week.

Oxtail Stew

My grandmother has always favored the cheaper cuts of meat, not only because she's trying to save a little money, but because she firmly believes they taste better. After enjoying a dish like this, you will be hard-pressed to argue. We also gauge how people like a dish by how much talking there is at the table. Well, with these oxtails there was hardly ever a peep. Serve accompanied by rice, pasta, or polenta.

Serves 4 as a main course

4 pounds oxtails, trimmed of fat and cut into 2-inch pieces

salt and pepper

$1/2$ cup all-purpose flour

2 tablespoons olive oil

3 slices bacon, cut into small pieces

1 onion, thinly sliced

1 clove garlic, crushed

1 carrot, peeled and diced

1 sprig fresh thyme

1 bay leaf

$1/2$ cup red wine

$1/2$ cup tomato paste, diluted with 1 cup water

4 cups chicken stock (see Basic Recipes, page 216)

1 cup peas, fresh or frozen

$1/2$ cup chopped fresh Italian parsley

Season the oxtail with salt and pepper. Dust the pieces of meat on both sides with the flour. In a heavy-bottomed pot over medium-high heat, sauté the meat in the olive oil, browning it well all over, approximately 2 to 3 minutes.

Remove the meat from the pot, then add the bacon to the oil and cook for 3 minutes, stirring frequently. Add the onion and garlic and sauté until soft. Add the carrot, thyme, bay leaf, and wine. Cook until the wine evaporates. Add the diluted tomato paste, chicken stock, and the browned oxtail and bring to a boil. Lower the heat, cover, and simmer for 1 hour or until the meat is tender. If it becomes too dry, add a little water.

After 1 hour, uncover, add the peas and parsley, cook for 5 more minutes. Remove to warm plates, spoon the sauce from the pan on top, and serve with rice, pasta, or polenta on the side.

Stuffed Artichokes

One of my grandmother's specialties is stuffed artichokes. I remember one Sunday, I had invited my *chef de cuisine* at Le Chantilly, Thomas Harris, over for dinner. After two and a half hours and five courses, Tom slumped in his chair waving the white flag of surrender. Little did Tom know that it was time for Nonna's artichokes. After getting just a whiff of them, he had to try one. Then, he had to go outside and lie down next to my German shepherd, Gino, to take a rest.

This appetizer or side dish is definitely meant to be eaten with the fingers so make sure there are plenty of napkins handy and an extra dish on the table to discard the inedible part of the leaves.

Serves 4 as an appetizer or side dish

4 large artichokes

½ cup lemon juice

4 cups water

5 tablespoons extra virgin olive oil

3 cloves garlic, minced

2 cups seasoned breadcrumbs (see Basic Recipes, page 219)

2 eggs, beaten

4½ tablespoons grated Parmesan cheese

2 tablespoons chopped fresh Italian parsley

freshly ground black pepper to taste

1½ cups chicken stock (see Basic Recipes, page 216)

Preheat the oven to 350° F.

Cut the stems from the bottoms of the artichokes, then cut ¼ inch off the tops. Rub liberally with the lemon juice so they don't discolor. Place the artichokes upside down in a saucepot in the water. Bring to a boil over medium-high heat and cook for 12 minutes. Remove from the pot and allow to cool. Pull out the inner cores of the artichokes, exposing the chokes. Scoop out the chokes with a teaspoon.

Heat the olive oil in a sauté pan over medium heat. Sauté the garlic until golden brown, about 2 minutes. Remove the pan from the heat and add the breadcrumbs, eggs, cheese, parsley, and pepper. Mix well, then stuff the mixture in the centers and in between the leaves of the artichokes. Place the artichokes in an 8 x 11-inch lasagna pan. Bring the chicken stock to a boil and pour it into the bottom of the lasagna pan. Cover with foil and bake for 40 minutes, or until the bottom leaves pull away easily. Remove the foil during the last 12 minutes. Serve hot.

Spinach Pie

Italian-Americans can take one vegetable and make it ten different ways. It goes back to the days when people had gardens or they went to seasonal markets. When the spinach was ready in the garden, you had enough to feed the family for the next couple of weeks. You didn't want to eat it the same way every night, so you had to be resourceful and find different ways to prepare it. My grandmother has so many recipes for spinach: she does ravioli, pies—open ones and closed ones—frittata, the list goes on. This is my favorite from her spinach repertoire.

Serves 6 as an appetizer, first course, or main dish

Dough

2 envelopes dry yeast

1½ cups plus 1 tablespoon warm water

4½ cups flour

2 teaspoons salt

Filling

3 pounds fresh spinach, stemmed and washed

$1/2$ cup pine nuts

$1/4$ cup extra virgin olive oil

$1/4$ cup minced onion

$1/2$ pound prosciutto, finely diced

4 cloves garlic, finely chopped

$1/4$ teaspoon crushed red pepper flakes

$1/2$ cup Gaeta olives, pitted and chopped

$1/4$ cup grated Parmesan cheese

$1/3$ cup white raisins

pinch of salt

Assembly

$3/4$ pound mozzarella cheese, shredded

2 tablespoons olive oil

1 egg plus $1/2$ teaspoon olive oil, mixed together

To make the dough: Dissolve the yeast in the warm water. Sift the flour and salt together. Place the flour mixture in a large bowl and mix in the yeast mixture and oil until a dough begins to form. Remove from the bowl and knead until smooth. Divide into two portions and place in two separate bowls. Cover with a cloth and keep in a warm area (at about 74° F) until they double in size.

Once the dough has doubled in size, place each piece on a lightly floured work area. Roll each into a 12 x 7-inch rectangle.

Preheat the oven to 350° F.

To make the filling: Steam the spinach for about 3 minutes, squeeze dry, and chop. Set aside.

Place the pine nuts on a cookie sheet and toast in the oven until golden brown. Set aside.

Bread and Soup

In my mind, soup is just soup. Sure, a good homemade recipe is better than what you get out of a can, but why not take it to the next level? If you really want to make it into something more substantial, make a real *zuppa* out of it—put a thick, crusty slice of Italian bread (toasted if you like) into the bowl and ladle the soup on top of it. It's no longer just "plain old soup," it's *zuppa*, a hearty, filling dish that can double as a first or main course for either lunch or dinner.

Heat the olive oil in a large pan over medium heat. Add the onion and cook until translucent. Add the prosciutto and cook for 2 minutes. Mix in the garlic, pepper flakes, and pine nuts. Cook for 1 minute more.

Add the reserved spinach. Lower the heat, fold in the Parmesan cheese, then add the raisins and olives. Cook for 1 minute more. Season with salt.

To assemble: Place one of the rectangles of dough onto a nonstick or lightly greased cookie pan. Top with the spinach mixture, sprinkle with the mozzarella, and drizzle with the 2 tablespoons of olive oil. Place the other rectangle of dough on top and pinch the edges. Brush with the egg mixture and bake for 35 minutes, until golden brown. Allow to cool for about 10 minutes, slice, and serve. The leftovers are good served at room temperature.

Migliaccio Napolitano

SAUSAGE, TOMATO, AND POLENTA CASSEROLE

Migliaccio in Italian slang means "to be better." (It's a colorful version of the word for better, *migliore;* you could translate it loosely as "more better.") I suppose this dish got its name because it makes a simple staple like polenta not only better, but terrific.

I had a great uncle, Tom, who lived in Far Rockaway, Queens, right on the water. We used to go to his house when we were kids and we would get soaked chasing each other with the horseshoe crabs that washed up on the beach. After 20 minutes of that on a cold day we were freezing, and Uncle Tom would warm us up with his *migliaccio.* My grandmother, Tom's sister-in-law, still makes a great *migliaccio.*

Serves 4 to 6 as a first course or main dish

Polenta

¼ **pound pancetta, cut into ⅛-inch dice**

8 **cups water**

1 **teaspoon salt**

2 **tablespoons butter**

2 **cups instant polenta**

1 **cup grated Parmesan cheese**

Sausage mixture

1 **tablespoon olive oil**

1 **onion, chopped**

1 **pound sweet Italian sausage, removed from casing and crumbled**

Assembly

1½ **recipes Garden Tomato Sauce (see Basic Recipes, page 217)**

½ **pound mozzarella cheese, shredded**

½ **cup grated pecorino cheese**

2 **tablespoons butter, softened**

Preheat oven to 375° F.

To make the polenta: Brown the diced pancetta in a small sauté pan until browned and reserve along with the drippings.

Place the water, salt, and butter in a large pot and bring to a boil. Simmer for 2 minutes. Remove the pot from the heat and quickly add the polenta while whisking vigorously. Place the pot back on the heat. Add ½ cup of the Parmesan and the cooked pancetta (with the drippings). Cook, stirring over medium-high heat for 5 to 6 minutes, until the polenta pulls away from the sides of the pan. Pour the polenta onto a small sheet pan lined with plastic wrap and spread evenly. Refrigerate for 20 minutes. Cut the cooled polenta into 5-inch squares. Discard the plastic wrap.

To make the sausage mixture: Place the olive oil in a sauté pan over medium-high heat. Add the onion and sauté until translucent. Add the sausage and cook until it is nicely browned. Reserve.

To assemble: Spoon half of the tomato sauce onto the bottom of an 11 x 17-inch lasagna pan. Top with a layer of half of the polenta. Sprinkle with half the mozzarella. Sprinkle a layer of half the sausage-onion mixture, then a layer of half the Parmesan and pecorino. Top with knobs of the softened butter using about half of it. Repeat with another layer of all the mixtures in the same order and finish with the remaining butter.

Bake for 30 minutes, or until it is lightly browned on top and bubbling on the sides. It's deliciously soupy so make sure you scoop it out of the pan with a big spoon and put plenty of the bubbly sauce from the pan on top of each portion.

Sweet and Sour Cippoline Onions

My great grandmother was never at a loss for words. She was a tough woman who could be blunt. She always said that a man had to eat a pound of *cippoline* before he could get married. In those days, we thought that was a punishment, but now these wonderful little onions are considered a delicacy. This dish, which is like a lightly pickled relish, makes a great appetizer, on its own or as part of an antipasto plate. It needs to be prepared several days in advance so it has time to pickle.

Cippoline means, literally, "little onions": they are sweet and delectable and are available, imported from Italy, in many stores and markets. If you can't find any, sweet Vidalia onions are an acceptable substitute or you can substitute regular, larger onions; just slice them thin.

Yields 4 quarts

2 cups water

2 cups white wine vinegar

1½ teaspoons salt

2½ pounds *cippoline* onions

2 tablespoons sugar

½ cup pine nuts

½ cup dried currants

freshly ground black pepper to taste

Place the water, vinegar, and salt in a deep sauce-pan over high heat and bring to a boil. Add the onions and cook for 4 to 5 minutes, until they are done but still firm. Remove the pan from the heat and stir in the sugar until it dissolves. Add the pine nuts, currants, and pepper. Ladle into a jar or any other airtight container. Allow to pickle for 3 to 4 days before eating. The onions can be placed in sterilized mason jars for future use or simply stored in the fridge in an airtight container for up to two weeks.

Potato and Rice Soup

When I was a kid, if I was sick, had a fever, had a cut, fell down in the street, fell off a truck—no matter what happened—my grandmother would say, "Eat this, you'll feel better." It didn't matter what tragedy occurred, you would always be consoled with, "Eat this, you'll feel better." More often than not, the remedy was this plain and simple soup.

Serves 4 as a first course, lunch, or snack

¼ cup olive oil

1 clove garlic, minced

1 onion, finely chopped

1 Idaho potato, peeled and diced into
    ½-inch cubes

1 cup white rice

2 cups chicken stock (see Basic Recipes, page 216)

1 tablespoon chopped fresh Italian parsley

1 tablespoon grated Parmesan cheese

Heat the olive oil in a saucepan over medium heat. Gently sauté the garlic, not allowing it to burn. Add the onion and potato and sauté for 2 minutes more. Add the rice and stock, then raise the heat and allow to come to a boil. Lower the heat and simmer for 1 hour, stirring occasionally. Add the parsley, stir in the cheese, ladle into bowls, and serve immediately.

Joe Generoso

Royal Crown Bakery

Revival of a Great Tradition

You could imitate their recipe, but it's more than just the dough that makes Royal Crown's bread great. With the old-fashioned stone-bottomed, brick-arched ovens, Giuseppe (Joe) Generoso, chief baker at Royal Crown, his brother Frank, and their staff turn out some of the best Italian bread in America. They operate out of two locations on 14th Avenue in Brooklyn, the pastry shop at No. 6512, and the bakery at No. 6308.

Building the ovens is almost a lost art. There are very few contractors who can still master the process of assembling the wood frame, positioning the bricks just so, and pulling out the frame so they fall in place perfectly, like an ancient Roman arch, with no masonry. The ovens are very large shallow arches. The one in the back of Generoso's pastry shop is 14 feet square and only 14 inches high; the one at the bakery a couple of blocks away is 18 by 14 feet and 30 inches high. It operates 24 hours a day at just over 600 degrees F. and can bake about 200 loaves at a time.

"The old ovens are a lot of work," Joe says. "You have to mop them out before you bake the bread in the morning and stoke them. Every time you bake a batch of bread, the oven cools down and you have to heat it back up again. The new ovens can turn out two to four times the amount of bread in the same space. They're metal, they have racks of stones to bake the bread on, gas burners, and constant temperature control. The bread is good, but it's not the same flavor. You can tell the difference." Royal Crown uses coal and oak wood to fire its ovens. Joe also burns some dried olive pits for just a small hint of that flavor.

Frank and Joe's original intention was to start their own pastry business in Brooklyn. In the late 1980s, they scraped together just enough money to buy one machine and get the oven going. The pastries sold, but everybody kept asking for bread.

"Bread came back," Joe says. "There was such a demand we had to start making it." What makes the bread so good? It's the ovens. It's the recipes.

It's the Generoso Brothers' constant care and supervision. It's also the spirit of the former owners. . . .

Joe remembers one stormy night in the early days when he was alone in the bakery at 2 A.M. making the dough. One of the machines went off; it was a blown fuse. Joe went down to the basement, replaced the fuse, then back upstairs to continue work. Within minutes, there was another blown fuse. He went down to investigate, fixed it, went back to work. After several more blown fuses, he finally got the problem fixed, turning off all but the essential machines. He was still working the dough by the light of one 20-watt bulb in the eerie silence, waiting for his brother Frank to show up, when he started to sense spirits flying around the room. "Sure, I was scared, but I knew I had to keep working," he says. "I didn't want to lose the dough. I called Frank again, then my mother, and told them to hurry up and come down to the bakery. The minute they got there, I told them what happened and then of course everything was okay."

Joe turns down plenty of requests to expand the

wholesale business because he doesn't want to compromise the hand-made quality of his product. "Making bread this way takes a lot of supervision," he says. "I've got to be there all the time to make sure everything is just right. It isn't just the money, it's the compliments, the feeling that we're doing something for people. We don't concentrate on volume, we just want our customers to be happy. If I go to a restaurant that we service and I see people eating our bread and enjoying their meal—that's what's important."

The basic product is a *pane di casa*, a large round peasant loaf with a crispy, crunchy, flour-dusted brown crust and a white, porous interior. There's the classic recipe and then a slightly softer variation. There's also *tortonno* or Crown bread, which is shaped like a big bagel; long bread, a baguette-shaped version of the *pane di casa*; and *pane antico*, a light sourdough made with slightly aged dough. There's still a line of pastry at the shop as well as about 30 other bread products, including olive sticks, prosciutto sticks, *grissini*

(occasionally), cheese sticks, and circular bread sticks called *taralli*. Royal Crown introduces a new product every six to eight months, a recent example being chestnut bread, which they sometimes bake with raisins if they feel the flour needs an extra sweetener.

berry reet

Although there are other New York City streets that I identify as Little Italy, Mulberry Street spells

Little Italy for millions of people. It's in the heart of Lower Manhattan,

between Houston Street and Canal Street, from Bowery to Lafayette. It's always been one of the

biggest Italian enclaves in the United States, primarily because New York City was the port of entry for almost all Italian immigrants, and a huge number simply stopped there. The large area that was Little Italy in the first half of this century has become much smaller as many of the immigrants have moved "up and out" in the world—that is, to the suburbs.

Manhattan's Little Italy has become more of a tourist attraction than a teeming neighborhood where people live and work, but the spirit remains intact and so does the cuisine. There are still plenty of restaurants, cafés, a few social clubs, and of course the street festivals.

For me and all of my friends and extended family, however, Little Italy means 18th Avenue in Bensonhurst, Brooklyn. It is here that you feel the warmth of the people and that you find the traditional Italian-American cooking—classic dishes like the ones that follow in this chapter. These are dishes that you should be able to find in any Little Italy anywhere in the world, but that are always more fun and more rewarding to cook at home. Just add a generous portion of your own love and enthusiasm and you'll bring Little Italy right into your own home.

Baked Mozzarella with Eggs

This is an easy and delicious recipe that makes a wonderful snack or luncheon dish. You can substitute any number of other cheeses for the mozzarella, including fontina or caciocavallo. Whatever you use, be sure to serve this dish with a good piece of crusty bread so you can mop up all the sauce.

Serves 4 as a snack or for lunch

1 cup Garden Tomato Sauce (see Basic Recipes, page 217), warmed

³/4 pound mozzarella cheese, cut into ¹/4-inch slices

8 eggs
salt and freshly ground black pepper to taste

Preheat the oven to 375° F.

Cover the bottoms of 4 single-portion oven-proof dishes with the tomato sauce. Top with equal portions of the sliced cheese and bake for 5 to 6 minutes. When the cheese starts to melt, break two eggs on top of the cheese in each dish, sprinkle with salt and pepper, cover with a piece of aluminum foil, and bake for an additional 2 to 3 minutes. Remove from the oven and serve right away.

Caponata Sicilian Style

A classic Italian-American recipe that makes an excellent appetizer or side dish for almost any meal. Caponata is also extremely tasty spread on a fresh piece of bread or as part of a sandwich for lunch or snacks. It will keep in your refrigerator well-wrapped for 3 to 4 days. Or you can follow my grandmother's fine example and make a huge batch and jar it.

Serves 6 as an appetizer or side dish

1 cup extra virgin olive oil

4 medium eggplants, peeled and cut into ¹/2-inch dice

4 medium onions, sliced

¹/2 cup tomato sauce

3 stalks celery, cut into ¹/4-inch dice

¹/2 cup capers, rinsed in water

15 green olives, pitted and cut into large pieces

1 tablespoon pine nuts, lightly toasted

¹/2 cup red wine vinegar

¹/4 cup sugar

³/4 teaspoon salt

¹/2 teaspoon white pepper

Heat the oil in a large skillet over medium heat and fry the eggplant until evenly browned, 3 to 4 minutes. Remove the eggplant from the skillet, leaving the oil. Sauté the onions in the oil for

about 6 minutes or until lightly browned. Add the tomato sauce and celery and cook for 4 minutes or until the celery is tender. Add a little water if necessary. Add the capers, olives, pine nuts, and cooked eggplant. In a separate saucepan, heat the vinegar and sugar until the sugar dissolves. Pour over the eggplant mixture and continue to cook for 20 minutes over low heat, stirring every 5 minutes. Season with the salt and pepper. Cool before serving.

Chicken Scaparello

CHICKEN WITH SAUSAGE AND PEPPERS

A lot of my friends from the old neighborhood in Brooklyn come to my restaurant Le Chantilly, which is a fancy place, but they don't always want to eat the kind of food we serve there. They want good old-fashioned peasant food, like Minestra or Chicken Scaparello. And sometimes they want to eat it like peasants. We can't have that at Le Chantilly, though; it might scare away our regular customers. So I just put my friends upstairs in the private room, serve them this dish, and everyone's happy.

Whatever you do, don't use boneless chicken. Chicken and fish are always more flavorful when cooked on the bone. Plus it's fun to use your hands a little bit when you eat. If you don't like to get your fingers sticky—forget about this recipe!

Serve accompanied by pasta or Parmesan Mashed Potatoes (page 33).

Serves 4 as a main course

1 4-pound chicken, cut into eighths

salt and pepper

$^{1}/_{4}$ cup olive oil

$^{1}/_{2}$ pound sweet fennel sausage, cut into 1-inch pieces

1 red onion, quartered, sliced $^{1}/_{4}$-inch thick and cut in half

1 whole head garlic, cloves separated and lightly crushed

1 red pepper, cut into 2 x $^{1}/_{4}$-inch strips

6 pepperoncini, stemmed and cut in half

2 cups chicken stock (see Basic Recipes, page 216)

1 cup brown veal (or beef) stock

$^{1}/_{4}$ cup plus 1 tablespoon red wine vinegar

1 teaspoon chopped fresh thyme

$^{1}/_{4}$ cup butter

$^{1}/_{4}$ cup fresh Italian parsley, chopped

Season the chicken with salt and pepper. Heat the olive oil in a large, ovenproof sauté pan or casserole. Add the chicken and cook over medium heat until it is crisp and nicely browned on all sides.

Remove the chicken from the pan and keep it warm.

Preheat the oven to 400° F.

Brown the sausage in the same pan that the chicken was cooked in. Add the onion and garlic and sauté for 1 minute. Add the red pepper and

pepperoncini and sauté for another minute. Pour in the chicken and veal stocks, $\frac{1}{4}$ cup of the red wine vinegar, and the thyme. Cover and roast in the oven for 25 minutes.

After 25 minutes, remove the pan from the oven and place it back on the burner over high heat. Allow the liquid to reduce by half. Stir in the remaining 1 tablespoon of vinegar, and add the butter and parsley. Remove the chicken and sausage pieces to warm plates, spoon the sauce on top and serve alongside Parmesan Mashed Potatoes.

Collari

CRISPY FRIED STUFFED BREAD

The Feast of Santa Rosalia, the Sicilian saint, is a marvelous tradition on 18th Avenue in Bensonhurst, Brooklyn. Every feast has its specialty food and this one is no exception. These little fried dough rolls stand out in my mind as the staple of the Santa Rosalia Festival. What a delectable snack!

Makes 12 sticks for appetizer or snack

Dough

1 envelope dry yeast

1 cup warm water

3 cups flour, sifted

1 teaspoon salt

$\frac{1}{2}$ cup lard, diced into $\frac{1}{4}$-inch cubes, at room temperature

Filling

$\frac{1}{4}$ pound thinly sliced prosciutto, cut into thin strips

$\frac{1}{4}$ pound sliced provolone cheese, cut into thin strips

15 pitted Calabrese olives, coarsely chopped

$\frac{1}{4}$ cup vegetable oil for frying

salt to taste

To make the dough: Dissolve the yeast in the warm water. Place the flour on a clean work surface and make a well in the center. Sprinkle the salt and scatter the lard pieces over the flour. Add the yeast mixture to the center of the well. Using your hands, gradually combine the flour-lard mixture with the yeast mixture until it is all well incorporated. Knead the mixture for 6 to 8 minutes, until you have a smooth dough. (This can also be done in a mixer using a dough hook.)

Place the dough in a lightly floured bowl, cover with a towel, and keep in a warm area. Allow the dough to double in size, approximately $1\frac{1}{2}$ hours.

Lightly flour the work surface. Take small pieces of the dough (about 2 tablespoons each) and roll each piece out into a 5 x $2\frac{1}{2}$-inch rectangle.

To fill: Alternate strips of prosciutto and provolone in the center of each rectangle of dough and sprinkle with 1 teaspoon of the olives, leaving a $\frac{1}{2}$-inch border. Roll it as you would a jelly roll. Dip your fingers in water and pinch the ends of the dough. Repeat the procedure until you have used all the dough.

Heat the vegetable oil to 375° F. in a deep, heavy-bottomed pot over medium heat. (If you

don't have a thermometer, you can take a small piece of dough and drop it in the oil to test it. The oil is ready when the dough comes right to the top and begins to fry.) Fry the *collari* a few at a time until golden brown on all sides. Drain on paper towels, sprinkle lightly with salt, and serve. *Collari* are best eaten right away.

Fried Calzones

Calzones are the familiar turnovers made from pizza dough and stuffed with cheese and meat or spinach that are found at the neighborhood pizzeria. "Calzone" literally means pants; maybe they get their name from the way they're folded over like a pair of pants.

This recipe is for a smaller, fluffier, tastier version of the same old-time favorite. Frying the calzones in olive oil gives them a wonderful flavor and aroma. They are great as an hors d'oeuvre or you can make a meal out of them.

Serves 8 as an appetizer, snack, or for lunch

1½ pounds pizza dough (see Basic Recipes, page 217)

¾ pound ricotta cheese

6 tablespoons extra virgin olive oil

½ cup diced baked ham or prosciutto (¼-inch dice)

½ cup shredded mozzarella cheese

freshly ground black pepper to taste

Start by dividing the dough into eight equal parts. Roll into balls, cover with a damp towel, and set aside.

In a bowl, mix the ricotta, 3 tablespoons of the olive oil, the ham, cheese, and pepper; set aside.

On a lightly floured work surface, flatten a ball of dough with your fingers or a rolling pin to a circle 5 inches in diameter and ⅛ inch thick. Repeat this procedure with all 8 balls of dough. Divide the filling and place equal portions on one side of each piece of dough. Fold the other half over and press the edges firmly closed to make a turnover shape. Repeat with the other pieces of dough.

Heat the remaining 3 tablespoons of oil in a frying pan big enough to hold two calzones. Fry them gently for 7 to 8 minutes until golden brown. Turn them once while cooking. Drain on paper towels and serve immediately.

Orecchiette with Broccoli Rabe

If broccoli rabe is too bitter for your taste, try increasing the blanching time by 2 minutes. The true Italian-American doesn't blanch it at all, in order to retain all of its flavor.

Although fresh pasta is better, you can also use dry orecchiette for this recipe.

Serves 4 to 6 as a first course or main dish

1 pound orecchiette

1 pound broccoli rabe, long stems removed

$1/2$ cup extra virgin olive oil

5 cloves garlic, chopped

8 anchovy fillets, rinsed and chopped

2 pepperoncini, seeded and chopped

$1/4$ cup grated pecorino cheese

$1/2$ teaspoon salt

Cook the orecchiette as instructed on the package.

Blanch the broccoli rabe in boiling salted water for 2 to 3 minutes until tender. Squeeze out the excess water.

Heat the olive oil in a large sauté pan over medium heat. Sauté the garlic in the oil, 1 to $1/2$ minutes. Add the anchovies and the pepperoncini. Cook, stirring, for 1 minute. Remove from heat, add the broccoli rabe and cooked orecchiette and toss. Sprinkle with the cheese, season with the salt, and serve immediately in warm bowls or dishes.

My Father's Nfigghiulata

STUFFED BREAD ROLL

My father is a better cook than he is willing to admit. He loves to tend his garden and cook what he grows there. Some of his bounty always finds its way into this tasty bread roll. In other parts of Italy and in many Italian-American neighborhoods, this dish is known as *stromboli*. In my father's native Sicily it's called by the colorful name *nfigghiulata* and takes on a more interesting form than *stromboli*. You can use many different vegetables, meats, or even cheeses for your filling, and it can be served as a hearty snack or an hors d'oeuvre or as a quick lunch with a salad on the side.

Serves 8 to 10 as an appetizer, lunch, or snack

Broccoli Rabe

Broccoli rabe has been part of Italian-American cooking for a long time but has only recently become widely popular. Legend has it that Andrew D'Arrigo, patriarch of Andy Boy in Salinas, California, America's largest broccoli grower, was responsible for developing the strain of broccoli rabe that most of us eat today.

In addition to blanching it for 2 to 3 minutes, you can cut the slightly bitter taste of broccoli rabe by dressing it with a little olive oil and lemon juice and/or by cooking it with a healthy dose of garlic. If you really like the bitter taste, try its Italian cousin, *cima di rabe.*

5 tablespoons extra virgin olive oil, plus more as needed

1 pound sweet Italian sausage meat, casings removed

1 medium onion, finely chopped

3 cups spinach leaves, stemmed and washed

5 scallions, coarsely chopped

1/4 cup Sicilian or Gaeta black olives, pitted and chopped

8 slices salami, cut into strips

4 very thin slices prosciutto, cut into strips

1/2 pound provolone cheese, cut into small dice

2 pounds pizza dough (see Basic Recipes, page 217)

salt and pepper to taste

Heat 1 1/2 tablespoons of the olive oil over medium-high heat in a skillet, add the sausage, and sauté for 2 minutes until lightly browned. Set aside in a bowl. In the same skillet, sauté the onion in 1 tablespoon of the olive oil for 2 to 3 minutes, until translucent. Add to the bowl of meat. In the same skillet, add 1 tablespoon of the olive oil and sauté the spinach until it wilts. Drain very well and squeeze dry. Set aside. In a separate bowl, mix the scallions, olives, salami, prosciutto, and cheese.

Grease an 11 x 17-inch jelly roll pan with 1 tablespoon of olive oil. Preheat the oven to 350°F.

On a floured surface, roll the pizza dough into a rectangle approximately the same dimensions as the prepared pan and 1/4-inch thick. Brush the dough with 1 tablespoon of olive oil. Leaving a 1-inch border, scatter all the prepared ingredients around the dough. Season with salt and pepper. Carefully roll the dough lengthwise, keeping it very compact. It should resemble a giant sausage. Make sure the roll is not loose when rolling. Pinch the ends so that the filling doesn't come out. Transfer carefully to the pan. Place seam side down on the prepared pan. Gently push the two ends to form a crescent shape. Brush with the remaining $1\frac{1}{2}$ teaspoons olive oil. Bake for $1\frac{1}{2}$ hours, brushing with additional olive oil every 15 minutes, until golden brown. If it starts to brown too fast, lower the heat to 325° F. Allow to cool, cut into thick slices, and serve.

Mozzarella in Carrozza

CRISPY CHEESE SANDWICHES

My grandmother is famous for this great afternoon snack. As a twist, she will slip in a slice of prosciutto or slices of green olives, or even some pieces of sun-dried tomato. You could even add some anchovy fillets, but always be sure to rinse them before chopping; otherwise, they're too salty. *Mozzarella in carrozza*, by the way, means "in a carriage," which is a nice way of saying between two pieces of bread.

Serves 6 for lunch or a snack

24 slices good bread, slightly larger in diameter than the cheese slices, crusts removed

1 cup milk

12 pieces of mozzarella cheese, approximately 3 inches in diameter and $\frac{1}{4}$-inch thick

1 cup flour, approximately, for dredging

3 eggs, well beaten with 1 teaspoon of salt and a pinch of pepper

1 cup breadcrumbs, approximately, for dredging

vegetable oil for deep frying

Moisten the slices of bread in the milk. Form sandwiches of bread, mozzarella, and, if you like, some of the ingredients my grandmother uses. Dredge in the flour, dip in the egg, then dredge in the breadcrumbs.

Pour oil to a depth of $\frac{1}{4}$ inch in a large sauté pan and heat over medium heat until 350° F. Fry the *carrozza* until golden brown on each side, drain on paper towels, and serve hot.

Pasta e Fagioli

PASTA AND BEANS

This is one of the best-known dishes in Italian-American cooking—"Pasta Fazool." My father says it's always better reheated on the second day and I agree. I have adapted my family's recipe and added a fancy touch, the oregano-rosemary oil.

Serves 4 as a first course or main dish

1½ cups dried cannellini beans

⅓ cup plus 2 teaspoons olive oil

3-ounce piece slab bacon

1 onion, chopped

11 cloves garlic, crushed

4 plum tomatoes, peeled, seeded, and chopped

8 cups chicken stock (see Basic Recipes, page 216)

salt and pepper to taste

4 ounces small pasta shells

3 sprigs fresh oregano

3 sprigs fresh rosemary

Soak the beans in water to cover overnight.

Heat 2 teaspoons of the olive oil in a large soup pot over medium heat. Cook the bacon in the olive oil until it starts to brown. Add the onion and cook for 2 to 3 minutes, then add 5 of the crushed garlic cloves and cook for 2 minutes more. Add the tomatoes and the chicken stock.

Rinse the soaked beans and add them to the pot. Season with salt and pepper and cook the soup until the beans are tender, approximately 1½ hours.

Cook the pasta shells as instructed on the package and set aside.

Once the beans are tender, remove the bacon from the pot. Also remove and reserve half of the cooked beans for garnish.

Ladle the remaining beans and liquid into a blender or food processor and puree until smooth. (If too thick, add a little hot chicken stock.) Check the seasoning. Mix in the reserved cooked pasta shells.

Heat the remaining ⅓ cup of olive oil in a small sauté pan over medium-low heat. Add the remaining 6 cloves of garlic and cook for 2 minutes. Then add the oregano and rosemary and sauté for 1 to 2 minutes. Strain and reserve the flavored oil.

Ladle the soupy puree into serving bowls. Sprinkle in some of the reserved beans. Drizzle with a spoonful of the oregano-rosemary oil and serve.

Pasta con la Mollica Catanese

SPAGHETTI WITH BREAD-CRUMBS CATANIA STYLE

This recipe is a tribute to my father's Sicilian origins. Catania is a town in Sicily whose people are resilient and find much happiness despite much hardship. Sicilian cuisine has great variety because the island has been conquered by so many different countries over the centuries and each conqueror has left behind a little of its culture.

Serves 2 as a first course or main dish

6 tablespoons olive oil

2 cups breadcrumbs

½ pound spaghetti

2 large cloves garlic, thinly sliced

2 small pepperoncini, chopped

1 bunch fresh Italian parsley, chopped

4 large tomatoes, peeled, seeded, and diced

6 tablespoons anchovy paste (if using whole anchovy fillets, rinse them before mashing up into a paste)

Preheat the oven to 350° F.

Heat 2 tablespoons of the olive oil in a sauté pan over medium heat and cook the breadcrumbs until nicely browned. Set aside, separating one quarter of the mixture.

Cook the spaghetti as instructed on the package and set aside.

Place the remaining 4 tablespoons of olive oil in a sauce pot over medium heat and sauté the garlic for 2 minutes; don't let it burn. Add the pepperoncini, parsley, and tomatoes and cook for 4 minutes. Remove from the heat and stir in the anchovy paste. Mix in the spaghetti, place the mixture in a casserole, and sprinkle the top with three-quarters of the breadcrumbs. Place the casserole in the oven for 2 to 3 minutes to set. Transfer to warm plates or dishes and serve immediately. Place the reserved breadcrumbs in a small bowl on the side to sprinkle on the pasta.

Pisarei with White Bean Sauce

Pisarei means "little peas." In this case, the little peas are actually miniature gnocchi the size of little peas. Gnocchi made this size are a great addition to your favorite soup. You can also freeze them for future use. Note that the beans need to be soaked overnight.

Serves 4 as an appetizer or first course

1½ cups dried Great Northern white beans

Gnocchi
2 cups all-purpose flour
1 cup fresh white breadcrumbs
1 cup milk
1 teaspoon salt
⅛ teaspoon freshly ground white pepper

Sauce
⅛ cup extra virgin olive oil
3 ounces pancetta, diced small
1 clove garlic, minced
1 carrot, peeled and finely chopped
1 stalk celery, finely chopped
1 onion, finely chopped
¼ cup dry white wine
2 cups peeled, seeded, and diced plum tomatoes
8 fresh basil leaves, chopped
¼ cup chopped fresh Italian parsley
salt and pepper to taste

Soak the beans in water to cover overnight.

To make the gnocchi: Mix the flour and breadcrumbs in a large mixing bowl. Add the milk, salt, and pepper and mix well. Knead the dough on a floured board until well blended. Divide the dough into three equal parts, allow to rest, covered, for 10 minutes. Take the dough and form into long, narrow cylinders, about ¼ inch in diameter. Cut the dough into small pieces the size of your pinky nail. Don't allow them to stick. At this point, you can freeze them for future use or cook them right away.

To make the sauce: Drain the beans and cook in enough salted water to cover by 1½ inches until tender, about 20 minutes. Heat the olive oil in a saucepan over medium heat and sauté the pancetta for 2 to 4 minutes. Add the garlic, carrot, celery, and onion. Cook for 7 to 8 minutes; do not brown. Add the wine and cook until it reduces by half. Add the tomatoes, drained beans, basil, and parsley. Season with salt and pepper, lower the heat, and simmer for 20 minutes.

When the sauce is almost done, bring a large pot of salted water to a boil over high heat. Drop the gnocchi in and cook for 4 to 5 minutes, or until they float. Drain well and place in dishes or bowls. Spoon the sauce on top and serve immediately.

Penne alla San Giovanni

PASTA WITH SAGE, WALNUTS, AND PROSCIUTTO

My very good friend Marc Bussio owns an Italian grocery store called Salumeria Biellese, which is on the West Side of Manhattan, around 29th Street and 9th Avenue. Marc is from the Piedmont area, northern Italy, where they have a completely different regional cuisine from what I'm used to among my Southern Italian and Sicilian relatives. Up north, they cook with plenty of what I would consider unusual ingredients. I would argue with Marc: "Are you crazy putting sage and walnuts with pasta?" But then I'd taste a dish like this and . . . well, you'll see for yourself. The flavors are a little bit out of the ordinary, but they combine beautifully in this delicious dish.

Serves 4 as a first course

1 pound penne

¼ cup extra virgin olive oil

5 cloves garlic, crushed

8 ounces prosciutto, sliced thin and finely diced

½ cup coarsely chopped walnuts

1 cup finely grated Parmesan cheese

salt and pepper to taste

½ cup butter

25 fresh sage leaves

Cook the penne as instructed on the package.

Heat the olive oil in a large sauté pan over medium heat. Add the garlic and cook until it starts to color, about 2 minutes. Add the prosciutto and continue to cook until the meat is browned. Add the walnuts and sauté for 1 to 2 minutes more. Remove from the heat.

Add the cooked pasta to the sauté pan and toss. Stir in the cheese. Season with salt and pepper. Place in a serving dish.

Heat the butter in a clean sauté pan and add the sage. Cook for 1 to 2 minutes. Spoon the sage-flavored butter over the pasta and serve.

Tripe with Red Beans

Tripe may not be at the top of everybody's list of favorite foods, but I like it on occasion and I recommend you try it. Since it's inexpensive, you'll see a lot of it in Italian-American cuisine. This is the best tripe recipe I know.

If you've never cooked tripe, don't worry about overcooking it. It's almost impossible to do so. Tripe looks a little like rubber and it's going to taste like it if you don't cook it long enough. Tripe is very tasty and makes for great eating in this recipe with red beans and cabbage.

Serves 4 as a first course or main dish

2 pounds tripe

2¼ teaspoons salt

5 stalks celery, 1 whole, 4 diced small

1 onion, stuck with 2 cloves

1 onion, thinly sliced

2 carrots, peeled and cut into ½-inch slices

2 tablespoons olive oil

¼ pound bacon, diced small

1 pound tomatoes, peeled, seeded, and diced large

pinch of saffron (optional)

1½ cups chicken stock (see Basic Recipes, page 216)

1 28-ounce can red beans, drained

½ small white cabbage, thinly sliced

3 large potatoes, peeled and cut into ¼-inch cubes

1 sprig fresh sage, chopped

3 tablespoons grated Parmesan cheese

freshly ground black pepper to taste

Place the tripe, 8 quarts of water, 2 teaspoons of the salt, the whole celery stalk, and whole onion in a large pot over medium heat and simmer for 2 hours. Remove the tripe from the pot and cut into thin strips. Discard the cooking liquid and vegetables.

In another pot over medium heat, place the sliced onion, carrots, diced celery, olive oil, and bacon, stirring until well browned. Add the tomatoes, tripe, remaining ¼ teaspoon salt, the saffron, and chicken stock and simmer for 10 minutes. Add the beans, cabbage, and potatoes and cook for 25 minutes more. Add the sage, cook for 5 minutes more. Sprinkle with the cheese and pepper, ladle into soup bowls, and serve.

Rigatoni alla Vodka

This is one of the ultimate Little Italy recipes. I can't prove it, but I believe this is a 100 percent original Italian-American dish. I don't believe it came from Italy, and I don't think it came from Russia either. It features Italian tomato sauce with vodka, a Russian drink that's made and consumed all over the world now.

You might ask: If it's such a common dish in so many restaurants, why include it in this book? For one thing, very few restaurants do it right. It simply cannot be made in advance; you must make it to order, otherwise you wind up with nothing but a tomato cream sauce. Here's how to make *Rigatoni alla Vodka* properly.

Serves 6 as a first course or 4 as a main dish

1 pound rigatoni

1 tablespoon olive oil

3 shallots, finely chopped

6 cloves garlic, finely chopped

4 ounces prosciutto, julienned

7 scallions, sliced, whites separated from the greens

⅛ teaspoon crushed red pepper flakes

¾ cup vodka

4 tomatoes, peeled, seeded, and diced

1 cup heavy cream

salt and pepper to taste

½ cup grated Parmesan cheese

Cook the pasta as instructed on the package.

Heat the olive oil in a large sauté pan over medium heat. Add the shallots, sauté for 1 minute, then add the garlic and cook until it begins to take on a light brown color. As soon as the garlic browns slightly, add the prosciutto and the whites of the scallions. Sauté for 2 minutes. Add the pepper flakes. Remove from the heat, carefully pour ¹⁄₂ cup of the vodka into the pan, and flambé. Add the tomatoes and the greens of the scallions as soon as the alcohol is evaporated and the flame has died. Add the remaining ¹⁄₄ cup of vodka and cook over medium heat for 15 minutes.

A note of caution: The key to flambéing is to remove the hot pan from the heat before you add the alcohol. Once you've added it, put the pan back on the heat, stand back, and allow it to ignite itself (if necessary, tip the pan a bit toward the heat, but don't light a match or lighter over it). Don't pour the alcohol in the hot pan while it's still on the burner; if you do, it will flare up in your face.

After 15 minutes, add the cream and continue to cook for 1 to 2 minutes more. Mix in the cooked pasta, season with salt and pepper, sprinkle with the Parmesan cheese, and serve immediately.

Ravioli Nudi

NAKED RAVIOLI

This dish gets its name from the fact that it is really the filling of the ravioli without the pasta. I guess somebody was feeling lazy, didn't want to bother making the pasta, and wound up with a new recipe. This dish offers the best of the ravioli without the heaviness of the pasta, so it's perfect for a light first course. Don't drown these delicate ravioli in tomato sauce. I recommend serving them with just a little butter spooned on top.

Serves 4 as a first course

¹⁄₂ pound ricotta cheese

2 pounds fresh spinach, center ribs removed, washed

5 extra-large egg yolks

³⁄₄ teaspoon grated lemon zest

1¹⁄₂ cups grated Parmesan cheese

pinch of cayenne pepper

salt and freshly ground black pepper to taste

1 tablespoon flour

¹⁄₄ cup butter

Drain the ricotta in a colander.

Blanch the spinach in a large pot of salted water over high heat for about 5 minutes. Drain and cool under cold water. Squeeze the spinach in a dish towel until completely dry. (If it is at all wet you will have problems later.) Chop the spinach very fine.

Combine the ricotta, egg yolks, lemon zest, 1 cup of the Parmesan, and the chopped spinach in a mixing bowl. Mix well and season with the cayenne, salt, and pepper. Add the flour and mix well.

To form the ravioli, wet your hands in cold water and, taking 1 tablespoon of the mixture at a time, form into little balls.

Bring a large pot of lightly salted water to a gentle boil over medium-high heat. Cook the ravioli in small batches until they float, about 2 minutes. Remove with a slotted spoon and place in a serving dish. Sprinkle with the remaining 1/2 cup Parmesan cheese. Melt the butter in a skillet and spoon over the ravioli. Serve immediately.

Penne al Forno con Melanzane

BAKED PASTA WITH EGGPLANT

Like many Italian-American families, mine has a certain number of recipes we like to make in bulk. This is one of them. It freezes very well; it's a lifesaver for single people, two-career couples, or anybody who doesn't have time to cook every day.

This dish can stand alone or be accompanied by a salad.

Serves 8 as a first course or 6 as a main dish

2 medium eggplants, peeled and sliced lengthwise 1/8-inch thick

salt

3/4 cup olive oil

1 pound penne

1 onion, chopped

2 cloves garlic, chopped

4 1/2 pounds tomatoes, peeled, seeded, and chopped

1/4 cup julienned fresh basil

2 tablespoons chopped fresh Italian parsley

salt and white pepper to taste

5 tablespoons butter, at room temperature

1 cup shredded mozzarella cheese

1 cup grated Parmesan cheese

Sprinkle the eggplant slices with salt and place in a colander to drain for 1 hour. Pat dry. Heat 1/2 cup of the olive oil in a large sauté pan over medium-high heat. Fry the eggplant in the hot oil on both sides until golden brown. Remove from the pan and reserve.

Cook the penne as instructed on the package. Preheat the oven to 375° F.

Heat the remaining 1/4 cup olive oil in a large pot. Add the onion and cook for 3 to 4 minutes until translucent. Add the garlic and sauté for 1 to 2 minutes. Add the tomatoes, basil, and parsley. Season with salt and pepper and cook for about 20 minutes over medium-low heat. Mix together with the penne.

Grease an 11 x 17-inch lasagna pan with 1 tablespoon of the butter. Layer half of the penne on the pan. Place a layer of half of the eggplant

Your Own Pizza Stone

You can bake pizzas on a regular cookie sheet or you can buy a pizza stone at a fancy gourmet supply store. Better yet, do what my grandmother did: Go to the masonry store and buy an unglazed tile the size of your oven rack. Soak it in water overnight, pat it dry with a towel, then place it in the oven before you turn it on to preheat. This allows the stone to heat up gradually to the full 450° F. without cracking.

over the penne, top with pieces of half of the remaining softened butter, half the mozzarella, and then sprinkle with half the Parmesan cheese. Repeat the layers.

Bake for 30 minutes. Scoop generous portions into plates or bowls.

Pizza Margherita

PLAIN TOMATO-CHEESE PIZZA

This is the one that just about everybody in America thinks of as the classic pizza. Americans might call it Pizza Napolitano, but in Italy, its correct name is Pizza Margherita. If you ask for a Pizza Napolitano over there, you'll get something completely different, like a white pizza without the tomato sauce.

Makes 2 12-inch pies

½ recipe pizza dough (see Basic Recipes, page 217)
1 pound very ripe plum tomatoes
salt
¼ cup tomato puree
8 fresh basil leaves, julienned
2 tablespoons olive oil
¼ pound mozzarella cheese, shredded
2 tablespoons grated Parmesan cheese

Prepare the dough as instructed in the basic recipe.

Peel, seed, and dice the tomatoes. Place them in a colander and sprinkle with salt, let drain for ½ hour. Place the tomatoes in a bowl with the tomato puree, basil, and olive oil.

Preheat the oven to 450° F.

Spoon the tomato sauce on top of the prepared dough, top with the mozzarella, and sprinkle with the Parmesan cheese. Bake on a pizza stone or cookie sheet for 12 to 15 minutes or until the edges are crispy. Serve immediately.

Salad of Rice, Tuna, Tomato, and Capers

This is a wonderfully colorful summer dish that has its roots in Sicily. Since it's surrounded by the sea, Sicily features many tuna dishes. My family would use canned tuna for this dish, but if you have access to fresh tuna, by all means use it (just cook it and incorporate it into the recipe).

Serves 6 as a side dish or for lunch

2½ pounds tomatoes, peeled and cut into ½-inch dice

1 teaspoon sugar

salt

2 6-ounce cans of solid white tuna

1 red onion, chopped

1 clove garlic, minced

2 tablespoons capers, rinsed

½ cup extra virgin olive oil

3 tablespoons fresh lemon juice

pinch of crushed red pepper flakes

2 cups cooked long-grain rice

¼ cup chopped fresh mint mixed with ¼ cup chopped fresh Italian parsley

Put the tomatoes in a colander and sprinkle with the sugar and salt. Set aside to drain for 20 minutes.

Drain the tuna, place in a bowl, and flake it with a fork. Add the onion, garlic, capers, olive oil, lemon juice, pepper flakes, and tomatoes. Mix well. Add the rice and herbs. Toss well. Allow to sit for at least one hour in the refrigerator. Toss again and serve.

This salad is good left over; simply cover the bowl with plastic wrap or place in an airtight container and refrigerate.

You've Got to Talk the Talk

I grew up in a well-known Little Italy in "Brookeleena." As you read this book, it won't take you long to realize that we have a language of our own—not only in my Little Italy but in every "Little Italy" in America.

For example, self-respecting Italian-Americans never called pasta "pasta"; it was always "macaroni." No matter what shape or form, it was always macaroni. Only nowadays, since Italian cooking has become so popular, do you hear people, even in my old neighborhood, refer to the stuff as pasta.

The centerpiece of Italian-American cooking, of course, is the "gravy." We never used the word sauce when we referred to tomato sauce for pasta; it was always the gravy for the macaroni. Today,

I find the fancy words "sauce for the pasta" almost alien.

There are also many dialect words used. "Scarole" was for escarole and sometimes for money, which also comes in green leaves. "*Canoul*" was for *cannoli*, and we always got a great laugh when we heard a non-Italian try to pronounce words like manicotti!

For those who speak "pure" Italian, the way we speak sounds different sometimes, maybe a little bit like slang. We would always say "*basingale*" for basil; "*cavateel*" for cavatelli pasta; "proshute" for prosciutto. So before you wander into Little Italy, practice your accent a bit so you can sound like a *paisan*, too.

Chapter Three

Shead Bay

Scungilli (conch), *calamari* (squid), shrimp, lobster, and of course fishing boats. This is the "Bay,"

my old stomping ground, where you encounter an **unforgettable**

aroma: the mixture of garlic, tomatoes, olive oil, and seafood that comes from some of the best

fish and shellfish dishes around. Sheepshead Bay is where I had my **first** restaurant job, at the Grotta D'Oro, at the end of **Emmon's** Avenue. Sheepshead Bay is basically a strip: one road—Emmon's Avenue—bordered on one side by a mile-long row of Italian restaurants and on the other by the **party** boats, which take groups of 50 or so fishermen out for the **day**. Every afternoon at 4:30, you can hear the party boats tooting their horns off in the distance as they return to the bay and the crowds waiting to buy the fresh fish right off the **boats**. Haggling over price is an art form practiced by many of the older Italian **women** out there.

Baccala Croquettes

When the Italians first came to America, *baccala* or salt cod was cheap peasant food. Because of that, every Italian woman worth her weight has many recipes for it. This is an interesting variation that is good served with some tomato sauce on the side for dipping.

Serves 4 as an appetizer or first course

1½ pounds salt cod

3 eggs

3 anchovy fillets, rinsed and chopped

1 tablespoon chopped fresh Italian parsley

½ teaspoon white pepper

2 tablespoons grated Parmesan cheese

2 slices white bread, soaked in water and squeezed dry

½ cup all-purpose flour

1 cup breadcrumbs

1 cup olive oil

Soak the cod in water for 24 hours, changing the water every 8 hours.

Place the cod in a skillet and cover with water. Bring to a boil over medium heat and cook for 30 minutes, then allow to cool. Bone, skin, and finely chop the cod. Beat 2 of the eggs. Combine the cod, anchovies, parsley, pepper, cheese, bread, and beaten eggs in a bowl and mix very well. Take 2 tablespoons of the mixture at a time and form into cylinder-shaped croquettes.

Beat the remaining egg in a shallow bowl. In 2 separate shallow bowls, place the flour and the breadcrumbs. Roll the croquettes, first in the flour, then the egg, and then lightly coat with the breadcrumbs. You can prepare the dish to this point the day before, then cover and refrigerate until you're ready to cook.

Heat the olive oil in a heavy-bottomed skillet over medium heat. Fry the croquettes until browned on all sides. This should take about 4 minutes on each side. Drain on paper towels and serve hot.

Baccala Neapolitan Style

Baccala as a winter holiday dish harks back to ancient seasonal traditions in Italy. In the late summer and fall, the codfish are running in the Mediterranean, and there is a large catch in Southern Italy. The cod isn't eaten right away, though; it's preserved in salt to be eaten in winter when most of the meat is gone.

This recipe is a superb main dish served with boiled potatoes or rice any time of year, but especially when the weather starts to get colder. This is a red version—with tomato sauce—whereas the recipe in Chapter 6 is a white version—with potatoes, olives, and onions.

Serves 4 as a main dish

1½ pounds salt cod

½ cup all-purpose flour

1 cup olive oil

3 cloves garlic, thinly sliced

2 tablespoons tomato sauce

¾ teaspoon crushed red pepper flakes

1 tablespoon capers, rinsed

12 black olives, pitted and cut into pieces

1 cup chicken stock (see Basic Recipes, page 216)

½ teaspoon white pepper

salt to taste

Soak the cod in water for 24 hours, changing the water every 8 hours.

Preheat the oven to 375° F.

Remove the skin and any bones from the cod. Roll the cod in the flour. Heat the olive oil in an ovenproof sauté pan over medium heat. Add the cod and fry until well browned on both sides. Remove from the pan and keep warm. Add the garlic to the same pan, lightly brown, and add the tomato sauce, pepper flakes, capers, olives, chicken stock, and pepper. Cook for 5 minutes. Add the fish to the pan and cover. Bake for 30 minutes. Season with salt if necessary, remove to a warm platter, and serve hot.

Fish Brodetto

FISH STEW

This dish is called a *brodetto*, which is halfway between a soup and a stew. You can make it in a regular soup pot, but it will taste even better in an earthenware terrine.

Serves 4 as a first or main course

½ cup extra virgin olive oil

1 onion, thinly sliced

2 cloves garlic, crushed

1 8-ounce can peeled Italian plum tomatoes, chopped, with the juice, or 4 fresh plum tomatoes, peeled, seeded, and diced

3 tablespoons tomato puree

1 teaspoon salt

½ teaspoon white pepper

¼ teaspoon crushed red pepper flakes

2 pounds mixed fish in season (sole, whiting, codfish, etc.), cut into 1½-inch pieces

1 small eel, peeled and cut into pieces (optional)

3 small squid, cleaned and cut into small rings

½ dozen littleneck clams, shelled, with the juice

1 tablespoon chopped fresh Italian parsley

1 teaspoon red wine vinegar

4 slices Italian bread, toasted

Heat the olive oil in a soup pot (or earthenware dish) over low heat and sauté the onion and garlic until the onion is translucent, about 3 to 4 minutes. Add the tomatoes, tomato puree, salt, pepper, and pepper flakes and bring to a boil. Add all the fish, except for the clams, and bring

back to a boil. Cover and cook for 20 minutes over low heat. Add water if necessary. (This is largely a matter of preference.) Uncover and add the clams with their juice, parsley, and vinegar. Cook for 3 minutes more. Place a slice of toast in each soup plate, ladle the soup on top, and serve, zuppa-style.

Crostini of Clams, Mussels, and Shrimp

Our family tradition was to spend Christmas Eve at my Uncle Ralph and Aunt Mary Claro's house. Aunt Mary was a terrific cook who made all the typical fish dishes—from fried eel to *polpo* (octopus), *baccala* (salt cod), and so forth. These *crostini* were always waiting after Christmas Eve mass. What a way to start a feast!

Crostini are small toasted pieces of bread, topped with a savory spread—an Italian-style canapé. Classic Tuscan *crostini* have a chicken liver topping.

Serves 6 as an appetizer

8 littleneck clams

8 small mussels

6 small shrimp, peeled and deveined

3 tablespoons extra virgin olive oil, plus more for brushing bread

3 cloves garlic

2 tablespoons chopped fresh Italian parsley

½ teaspoon crushed red pepper flakes

2 plum tomatoes, peeled, seeded, chopped, and drained

2 tablespoons dry white wine

24 slices Italian bread

Scrub the shellfish clean. Heat 2 tablespoons of the olive oil in a heavy pot over medium heat. Place the clams and mussels in the pot and cover. The shells should open in about 7 to 10 minutes. (Discard any that don't.) Strain and reserve the liquid. Remove the shellfish from the shells and discard the shells. Dice the shrimp, clams, and mussels.

Chop 1 clove of the garlic and sauté in the remaining tablespoon of oil in a skillet over medium heat; do not let it brown. Add the shellfish, parsley, and pepper flakes. Cook for 2 minutes. In a separate pot, combine the tomatoes, wine, and reserved shellfish broth over medium heat. Cook for 3 to 4 minutes, until thickened. Add to the shellfish and cook for 2 more minutes. Remove from the heat.

Rub the bread with the remaining 2 garlic cloves and brush with olive oil. Arrange in a single layer on a sheet pan and toast both sides. Top each piece of toast with a portion of the seafood mixture, arrange on a platter, and serve warm.

Spedini di Polpo e Calamari

BROCHETTES OF OCTOPUS AND SQUID

In my family, life revolves around tradition. One of my favorite traditions is the summer barbecue —not exactly exclusive to Italian-Americans, but the ingredients we use surely are. Brooklyn is surrounded by salt water. My family in Italy is close to the sea. So you can understand why we cook a lot of fish. This seafood dish, which will make an impressive addition to your barbecue repertoire, can be prepared ahead of time. Just put it in a baking pan or glass dish, cover with plastic wrap, and store in the fridge until you're ready to fire up the grill.

Serves 6 as an appetizer or main dish

Brochettes

4 pounds squid

4 pounds medium octopus

6 slices white bread, crust removed

2 tablespoons chopped fresh basil

2 tablespoons chopped fresh Italian parsley

2 cloves garlic, chopped

¼ cup extra virgin olive oil

salt and pepper to taste

Sauce

1 cup olive oil

2 cloves garlic

¼ cup fresh basil leaves

salt and pepper to taste

To make the brochettes: Clean the squid by removing any dark skin from the outside, the cartilage, and the innards. Wash well under cold water. (Squid can also be bought pre-cleaned at your local fish market.)

Wash the octopus under cold water, then parboil it in unsalted water over medium heat for 20 minutes. Remove the octopus from the water and pull off the purplish skin while still hot. (It comes off easily.)

Chop the bread coarsely in a food processor. Place in a mixing bowl and add the herbs, garlic, olive oil, and salt and pepper. Mix until it is the consistency of a paste.

Cut the octopus and squid into ½-inch pieces and skewer, alternating the two. Spread the bread mixture in a pan and roll the brochettes in it to cover evenly.

Prepare a charcoal grill. Cook the brochettes on the grill over low heat for 7 minutes, turning periodically so they are evenly cooked.

To make the sauce: Put all the ingredients for the sauce in a blender and blend until the mixture is smooth. Place the brochettes on a warm platter, spoon the sauce on top of the cooked brochettes, and serve.

Clams by Size

Hard-shell clams are categorized by size. When they are under two inches in diameter, they're called littlenecks. Clams between two and three inches in diameter are cherry-stones. Clams larger than that are called chowder clams or quahogs.

Clam stuffed Mushrooms

In Sheepshead Bay, there used to be a place called Joe's Clam Bar. This was our Friday night hang-out after going out. They made these mushrooms as part of their hot antipasto. Joe's Clam Bar is gone now, but its great stuffed mushrooms live on.

Serves 6 as an appetizer

18 large mushrooms

1 dozen littleneck clams, washed under cold water (you may substitute canned, minced clams if fresh aren't available or if you want a shortcut)

$1/4$ cup white wine

3 tablespoons extra virgin olive oil

3 cloves garlic, minced

1 cup fresh breadcrumbs

3 tablespoons chopped fresh Italian parsley

1 teaspoon chopped fresh oregano

salt and pepper to taste

1 lemon

Remove the mushroom stems, mince them finely in a food processor and reserve. Leave the caps whole.

Place the clams and the wine in a skillet over medium heat. Cover and allow to steam for 3 to 4 minutes until the clams are open. (Discard any that don't open.) Mince the meat from the clams, discard the shells, strain the juice from the pan and reserve.

Preheat the oven to 425° F.

Heat 2 tablespoons of the olive oil in a skillet over medium heat. Sauté the garlic in the oil for 2 minutes; do not let it turn brown. Add the reserved chopped mushroom stems and cook for 2 minutes more. Remove from the heat and add the clams, breadcrumbs, parsley, and oregano. Season to taste with salt and pepper. Mix well.

Stuff the mushroom caps with the mixture, then drizzle them with the remaining tablespoon of olive oil. Bake for 15 minutes. Remove from the oven, squeeze some fresh lemon juice over the mushrooms and serve.

Spinach Linguine with Zucchini and Shrimp

This is a terrific summer dish. It's fresh and light, and zucchini is a quintessential summer vegetable. You can find dry spinach pasta at most stores if you prefer not to make it fresh. You can also substitute regular linguine or fettucine if you like.

Serves 6 as a first course or main dish

2 small zucchini, cleaned

coarse sea salt

$1/2$ pound small shrimp, unshelled

1 lemon

$1/4$ cup olive oil

1 large clove garlic, coarsely chopped

large pinch of saffron

1 cup very warm chicken stock (see Basic Recipes, page 216)

salt and freshly ground white pepper

1 large tomato, blanched, seeded, and cut in large dice

15 sprigs fresh Italian parsley, leaves only

1 recipe spinach linguine (see Basic Recipes, page 218)

Cut the zucchini into disks not more than $1/8$-inch thick and let them stand for 30 minutes in a bowl of cold water to which coarse salt has been added.

Place the shrimp in a bowl of cold water with coarse sea salt. Cut the lemon in half, squeeze the juice into the bowl with the shrimp and salt. Place the lemon in the bowl and let soak for 30 minutes.

Drain the zucchini and rinse under cold water. Drain the shrimp, and shell and devein them.

Place a pot of cold water over medium heat for the pasta.

To prepare the sauce: Heat the oil in a skillet over low heat and sauté the garlic for 2 minutes. Dissolve the saffron in the chicken broth.

Add the zucchini to the skillet and cook for 30 seconds, then raise the heat to high, season with salt and pepper and add the broth. Cover the skillet and cook 2 minutes, stirring every so often with a wooden spoon. Add the shrimp and tomato to the skillet, mix well, and cook for another 2 minutes.

When the pasta water reaches a boil, add some coarse sea salt, then the pasta, and cook for 2 to 3 minutes. Drain the pasta, add it to the skillet, sprinkle with the parsley, mix well, transfer to a warm platter, and serve.

Roasted Peppers Stuffed with Squid

I remember years ago when everybody would fish for squid in Sheepshead Bay by putting lightbulbs upside down in the water at night. (As anyone who's spent time around the shore knows, most sea creatures are attracted to lights at night, like moths to a flame on a summer night.) The squid would come swimming up so it was easy to net them. There would be an abundance of squid, and there's just so much fried calamari and you can eat. At the same time, the peppers would be starting to ripen. We would never grow just six pepper plants; we'd grow sixty. So there was an abundance of peppers, too. Too many peppers, too much squid. It was fate that the two would come together.

Serves 6 as a first course

1¼ cups olive oil

1 eggplant, peeled and diced large

1 clove garlic, slightly crushed

½ cup breadcrumbs

2 cloves garlic, chopped

6 tomatoes, peeled, seeded, and diced

½ cup flour

2 small squid with tentacles, diced small (see cleaning instructions on page 88)

¼ cup tomato paste

½ teaspoon salt

pinch of pepper

1 cup pitted black olives, cut in half

1 bunch fresh Italian parsley, chopped

1 tablespoon capers, rinsed

6 large red peppers, cored, tops reserved

Heat ¼ cup of the olive oil in a large sauté pan over medium heat and brown the eggplant. Drain on paper towels and reserve.

In the same pan, heat 1 tablespoon of olive oil over medium heat and cook the crushed garlic clove until lightly browned. Discard the clove and add the breadcrumbs to the garlic-flavored oil. Once toasted, remove the breadcrumbs from the pan and reserve.

Heat ¼ cup olive oil in the sauté pan over medium heat. Sauté the chopped garlic until golden brown, then add the tomatoes and cook for 2 minutes. Remove the mixture from the pan and set aside.

Preheat the oven to 325° F.

Flour the squid and sauté in 3 tablespoons of oil in a skillet over high heat until nicely browned. Set aside.

Dilute the tomato paste in ¼ cup water, add ¼ cup olive oil and season with the salt and pepper. In a saucepan over medium-high heat, cook the sauce until it thickens, about 8 to 10 minutes. Set the sauce aside.

In a bowl, combine the diced tomato mixture, eggplant, breadcrumbs, squid, 2 tablespoons of cooked tomato sauce, olives, parsley, and capers. Adjust the seasoning. Stuff the peppers with the mixture and put their tops back on.

A Word About Tuna

Like many fresh ocean fish, tuna can be very expensive. Big-eye tuna is the top of the line, hard to obtain, and very expensive. Yellowfin is a more common type of tuna that works very well. But try to find fresh bonita, if possible. It's a smaller fish, darker, very tasty, and less expensive than its bigger cousins.

Place 2 tablespoons of the olive oil in an oven-proof glass dish or metal roasting pan big enough to hold all the peppers. Take half of the reserved remaining sauce and spoon it onto the bottom of the dish. Place the peppers upright in the dish, top each with a spoonful of sauce and bake in the oven for 45 minutes to an hour. The peppers should be tender, cooked, but not overdone to the point where they fall apart. Remove them from the dish carefully with a spoon—they are delicate—and place onto serving plates.

Grilled Tuna Castelle al Mare

Castelle al Mare is the beautiful oceanfront town in Sicily my father comes from. It is known for its seafood, including fresh tuna. This particular way of preparing tuna is simple and elegant and brings out the best in a good fresh piece of fish.

When you buy tuna, always look for pieces with a deep, rich red color, preferably center-cut. Then take them home and cook them this way. If you plan to leave them in the fridge for any time, put them in a pan or bowl on a bed of ice. Make sure they're well wrapped in plastic wrap or wax paper, though, so the ice doesn't damage the flesh.

Serves 6 as a main dish

Marinade

5 tablespoons olive oil

3 tablespoons lemon juice

pepper to taste

5 sprigs fresh oregano

6 tuna steaks, cut 1 inch thick

Sauce

$^1/_2$ cup chopped fresh Italian parsley

2 tablespoons chopped fresh oregano

$^1/_3$ cup extra virgin olive oil

$^1/_2$ cup scallions, sliced

2 tablespoons capers, rinsed

$^1/_2$ cup pepperoncini, seeded and chopped

$^1/_4$ cup lemon juice

To make the marinade: Mix all the ingredients for the marinade and place with the tuna in a glass or plastic container. Refrigerate for 30 minutes.

Preheat the grill or barbecue. Mark the tuna on the grill, 1 minute per side.

To make the sauce: Combine all the sauce ingredients in a large sauté pan over medium heat. Add the tuna and cook at a low simmer for 2 minutes. Do not allow the liquid to come to a boil. (*Note:* Cooking the tuna for 2 minutes will result in medium-rare; 3 to 4 minutes, medium; 5 to 6 minutes, well-done.)

Remove the tuna from the pan to a platter, top with the sauce and serve immediately.

Sea Snails in Tomato Sauce

When you mention snails in relation to Italian cooking, many people think of *scungilli*, which are actually conch. My mother's family from Naples calls the small sea snails *lumachine*, "little snails." My father loves them, and being Sicilian, he refers to them as *babaluci*. If you can't find them fresh in their shells, used canned escargots.

Serves 2 as a first course

$^3/_4$ cup olive oil

1 large onion, chopped

5 cloves garlic, minced

1 pound ripe tomatoes, peeled and chopped

1 7-ounce can snails or 1 pound fresh snails in the shell

1$^1/_2$ teaspoons salt

1 cup chopped fresh Italian parsley

$^1/_2$ cup white wine

2 to 3 teaspoons crushed red pepper flakes

4 thick slices Italian bread, toasted

Heat the olive oil in a skillet over medium-high heat and sauté the onion and garlic for 4 to 5 minutes until translucent. Add the tomatoes and cook, uncovered, for 8 to 10 minutes, until the sauce thickens. Add the snails, salt, parsley, wine, and pepper flakes. Cook for 8 minutes more. Place the toasted Italian bread in dishes or bowls, ladle the snails on top, and serve. If you used the fresh snails, don't forget to pick them up and suck: the snail will come right out.

Spaghetti with Crabs

I love to go after blue crabs in the summer with my sons Anthony and Paul. I love to eat spaghetti with crabs even more. The crabs make a delicious gravy for the macaroni. My grandmother insists that you must clean the crabs when they are alive, but be careful because their claws are very sharp. If you prefer, you can blanch the crabs in boiling water for 2 minutes and then follow the instructions for cleaning.

Serves 6 as a first course or 4 as a main dish

4 live blue crabs (or any other hard-shell crab such as Dungeness, Maine, etc.)

¼ cup extra virgin olive oil

3 large cloves garlic, crushed

¼ teaspoon crushed red pepper flakes

3 pounds plum tomatoes, peeled, seeded, and finely diced

salt and pepper to taste

1 pound spaghetti

¼ cup chopped fresh Italian parsley

Start by cleaning the crabs (see note above). Pull the large back shell off. Clean all the debris from the center and discard. Cut the body into 4 pieces, using a heavy knife to go through the shell. Crack the claws and legs once each with a hammer or nutcracker.

Heat the olive oil over medium-high heat in a large, wide pan. Sauté the garlic for 2 minutes; do not burn. Add the crabs and sauté for 2 minutes more. Add the pepper flakes, tomatoes, salt, and pepper. Allow to come to a simmer, lower the heat, and cook for 15 minutes.

Meanwhile, cook the spaghetti al dente, as instructed on the package. Drain the pasta and put it on a warm platter. Stir the parsley into the sauce, spoon the crabs and sauce on top of the spaghetti and serve. Make sure you have nutcrackers, plenty of napkins, and an extra dish for the discarded shells on the table.

Philomena's Stuffed Calamari

STUFFED SQUID

Aunt Angie, my grandmother, and their friend Philomena make regular trips to Atlantic City and, believe it or not, they never lose. They play only the slots and they have a terrific system. They post themselves at strategic lookouts around the slot machine area. When someone's ready to get up after putting a lot of coins in a particular machine, the signal goes out and the ladies pounce. Philomena is particularly good at this system. She also has a great system for making stuffed squid. If you don't have the patience to sew them up like she does, you can always skewer them with a toothpick. Instructions for cleaning the squid are included but if you find this too complicated or time-consuming, just buy the squid precleaned from your fish market. This dish is delicious served on a bed of linguine.

Serves 4 as an appetizer or main dish

6 large squid

Stuffing

3 tablespoons olive oil

3 cloves garlic, minced

6 squid tentacles, diced

1 bunch fresh Italian parsley or chervil, chopped

½ teaspoon Italian seasoning, or you can use a mixture of chopped fresh thyme, rosemary, and a bay leaf

¼ cup pine nuts, toasted

¼ cup raisins

2 eggs

1½ cups diced Italian bread (¼-inch cubes)

¾ cup grated Parmesan cheese or ¼ cup grated pecorino

½ teaspoon salt

¼ teaspoon pepper

Sauce

3 tablespoons olive oil

2 cloves garlic, lightly crushed

¼ cup white wine

1 28-ounce can crushed tomatoes with juice

1 tablespoon tomato paste

1 4-ounce bottle clam juice

2 teaspoons sugar

½ teaspoon Italian seasoning

1¾ cups chicken stock (see Basic Recipes, page 216)

1 bunch whole fresh basil

To clean the squid: Remove the "plastic," which is the cartilage. Wash the inside and then cut the tentacles between the eyes and the arms to remove the lower part with the mouth and eyes.

To make the stuffing: Heat the olive oil in a large sauté pan over medium heat. Sauté the garlic and squid tentacles for about 3 minutes. Add the parsley, Italian seasoning, nuts, and raisins. Stir well and set aside to cool. Once the pan and the squid mixture cool, add the eggs, bread cubes, cheese, salt, and pepper and mix well.

Stuff the cleaned squid with the stuffing mixture (don't overstuff because squid will shrink slightly), then sew the open lip with a needle and thread. (Make sure you leave about $1/2$ inch of thread and don't make a big knot so that you can pull the string out later.)

Preheat the oven to 375° F.

To make the sauce: Heat the olive oil in a metal casserole over medium heat. Toss in the garlic and sauté on low heat for about 1 to 2 minutes. Add the stuffed squid to the pan carefully and allow them to brown lightly. If the garlic begins to burn, remove it. Add the wine and let it reduce a little. Remove the squid. Throw out any garlic left in the pan, then continue to cook the wine until it's reduced by three-fourths. Add the tomatoes, tomato paste, clam juice, sugar, and Italian seasoning. Stir well and let simmer for about 20 to 25 minutes on low heat. Add the chicken stock, basil, and squid. Let it come to a boil, cover with aluminum foil, and bake for about 45 minutes. Remove the string from the squid and serve on a bed of linguine, spooning the sauce on top.

Cleaning Sea Snails

If you collect sea snails yourself on the beach, they need to be cleaned because they tend to ingest anything and everything from the water around them. We used to layer the bottom of a cardboard box with baking soda and leave the snails in there. They would consume the baking soda, cleaning themselves out. If you buy the snails fresh from the market, they have already been treated and all you need to do is rinse them with cold water.

Stufato of Swordfish and Shellfish

SWORDFISH AND SHELLFISH STEW

Stufato means stew in Italian. This dish is a great example of marrying swordfish, which has a tendency to be somewhat bland, with flavorful shellfish. When selecting ingredients for this recipe, look for the most unusual shellfish you can find. When I was a kid we used to go to Jamaica Bay and look for *lumachine di mare*, which are the tiny sea snails that cling to the sides of the piers. We used to remove them from their shells with a toothpick. *Lumachine*, mussels, and razor clams are terrific in this recipe.

Serve the stew with crusty bread if it's a first course, or rice, boiled potatoes, or your favorite fresh pasta if it's a main course.

Serves 4 as a main course

¾ cup extra virgin olive oil

5 cloves garlic, crushed

5 pounds assorted shellfish (mussels, clams, razor clams, snails, etc.), washed well under cold water

1½-pound swordfish steak, without skin (center cut is preferable)

salt and freshly ground black pepper to taste

½ small white onion, chopped

15 black olives, pitted

1 pound plum tomatoes, peeled, seeded, and diced

1 sprig fresh rosemary

2 tablespoons chopped fresh Italian parsley

Place 5 tablespoons of the olive oil, the garlic, and the shellfish in a deep pot over medium-high heat. Cover and cook for 4 to 5 minutes, stirring frequently, until all the shellfish have opened. (Discard any that don't open.) Remove the shellfish and keep warm. Strain the liquid using a fine sieve, cheesecloth, or a coffee filter. Reserve.

Season the swordfish with salt and pepper. Heat 1½ tablespoons of olive oil in a skillet over high heat and cook the swordfish until golden brown, about 2 minutes on each side. Remove from the pan. Add 4½ tablespoons olive oil to the same pan, then add the onion and cook for 3 to 4 minutes over medium heat. Add the olives, tomatoes, rosemary, swordfish, and shellfish liquid. Cover and cook for 7 minutes. Add the cooked shellfish and cook for 5 minutes more. Finish with some freshly ground pepper and the parsley. Ladle into bowls and serve hot.

A Word About Skate

Skate is the edible member of the ray family, related to the sting ray, electric ray, and giant manta ray. Its flesh is white, firm, and tasty, similar to that of shark or scallop. Be sure the skate is very fresh. If it's kept for any length of time, it starts to develop a strong ammonia smell. When you buy skate, you can have your fishmonger remove the skin since that's where most of the ammonia is concentrated. This is also advisable because the skin is very tough.

Linguine with Skate Sauce

In the course of bottom fishing for flounder, blackfish, or porgies off the party boats from Sheepshead Bay, we would often pull in skate. Most people would throw it right back, except for the Italians, who knew it was a delicious piece of seafood. Now, at least 20 years later, skate is a very popular item at some choice restaurants, and of course no one would think of throwing it back anymore. If you buy the skate at a market instead of catching it yourself, ask your fishmonger to skin and bone it for you.

Serves 4 as a first course, 2 as a main dish

¾ **pound skate, skinned, and boned**

12 ounces linguine

5 tablespoons extra virgin olive oil

3 cloves garlic, minced

1 tablespoon chopped fresh Italian parsley

1 tablespoon chopped fresh basil

6 ounces fresh plum tomatoes, peeled and coarsely chopped

salt and pepper to taste

Parboil the skate in salted water to cover, simmering it for about 12 minutes after it comes to a boil. Remove it from the water and set aside.

Cook the linguine al dente as instructed on the package.

While the pasta is cooking, heat the olive oil in a large sauté pan over medium heat. Add the garlic and cook for 1 minute; do not let it brown. Add the skate, crumbling it into the pan (it will break up easily after parboiling), the parsley, basil, tomatoes, salt, and pepper. Toss well, lower the heat and simmer for 10 minutes. Add the linguine to the pan and toss. Transfer equal portions to warm plates and serve.

mo's arden

Vegetable gardens are a tradition in the Italian-American family. My father still plans his entire year around his garden. I have fond memories of Mimmo, one of my best **friends** from the old neighborhood, who made his living going around and cutting people's lawns and selling **tomato** plants. Like many Italian-Americans, he also grew his own vegetables. All summer, whenever anybody passed by, they would be sure to check on how Mimmo's garden was doing.

Because he was so good at growing things, by the end of the summer Mimmo would always have an abundance of produce. He had to find ways to use it all. His **wife** was a terrific cook and so was he. But the two of them could never work in the kitchen at the same time. When they did, you could hear them screaming at each other from the street.

Mimmo made a lot of things that people take for granted today. Everybody talks about sun-dried tomatoes nowadays, but he made them years before they were chic. He would take the Italian plum **tomatoes** from his garden, cut them in half, dry them in his backyard in the hot summer sun, and preserve them. He would can **vegetables**, dry them, or salt them. He even used plants that grew wild in his yard. He could always locate the best dandelion greens. Mimmo's vegetables preserved in oil, such as smoked peppers **stuffed** with anchovies and breadcrumbs, were incredible.

This chapter is dedicated to Mimmo and to all the great garden-vegetable recipes he inspired.

Barbecued Artichokes

I call these artichokes barbecued, but actually you can do them either on the barbecue or in the fireplace because you put them directly into the burning embers. When I was a kid, we had huge grapevines in our backyard. In the fall when the grapes were picked, my grandfather would cut back the vines and burn the cuttings in the yard. The artichokes cooked on those grapevine fires were delicious.

Serves 6 as an appetizer or side dish

6 medium artichokes, washed, trimmed of lower leaves, stems trimmed flat

1 cup extra virgin olive oil

salt and freshly ground black pepper to taste

1½ tablespoons crushed red pepper flakes

1 cup *bagna cauda* (see Basic Recipes, page 216), for dipping

Start by making a fire of hardwood or of a hardwood charcoal such as mesquite. Do not use commercially made briquettes; they contain chemicals and your food will taste like them.

Stand the artichokes up and with the heel of your hand push down to open up the leaves. This will enable you to get all the ingredients inside. Drizzle the artichokes with the olive oil inside and out. Sprinkle the salt, pepper, and pepper flakes liberally inside and out.

Wait until the flames have died down and the fire consists of glowing embers. Rearrange the embers, making wells or spaces among them. With long tongs, place the artichokes in the wells. Gently push the embers back around the artichokes without completely covering them. Cook the artichokes for 45 minutes or until tender. You can check for doneness with a long skewer, making sure they are tender. Remove from the fire and place on a towel. Pull off the burnt outside leaves and discard them. Eat the rest.

Ciambotta

VEGETABLE STEW

Ciambotta is like a vegetable compote. It's the Italian version of the famous French dish ratatouille. This dish comes from the region in and around Naples, and offers a great way to use some of the bounty from your kitchen garden or the fresh produce from your favorite vegetable market. It goes particularly well with grilled fish or meat.

Serves 6 as an appetizer or side dish

½ cup olive oil

3 cloves garlic, crushed

3 onions, diced

1 red pepper, diced

2 yellow peppers, diced

1½ pounds canned tomatoes, diced large

1 pound potatoes, diced small

1 eggplant, peeled and medium dice

1 zucchini, medium dice

8 green olives, pitted and sliced

1½ teaspoons salt

½ teaspoon pepper

½ cup julienned fresh basil

Heat the oil in a large sauté pan or large casserole over medium heat. Add the garlic and cook until it turns a light golden color. Lower the heat. Add the onions and cook until they are translucent. Add the peppers, cover, and cook for about 2 to 3 minutes. Add the tomatoes, potatoes, eggplant, zucchini, olives, salt, and pepper. Continue to cook the mixture over low heat until all the vegetables are tender, about 10 minutes. Sprinkle in the basil and serve.

This dish can be kept in the fridge for several days and is great as a leftover, served at room temperature, or reheated if you like.

Carciofi alla Judea

FRIED ARTICHOKES
JEWISH STYLE

Jewish culture has influenced Italian cooking, especially around Rome where there has traditionally been a Jewish population. This simple, elegant preparation intensifies the delicious flavor of the artichokes.

Serves 4 as an appetizer, first course, or side dish

4 medium artichokes

juice of 1 lemon

1 teaspoon salt

freshly ground black pepper to taste

3 cups olive oil

Remove the tough outer leaves of the artichokes, peel the stalk, and cut off the sharp tips of the leaves with a scissors. Turn the artichokes so they're stalk side up and press down hard to flatten and spread the leaves open. Wash them and sprinkle with lemon juice. Season the insides with the salt and plenty of pepper. Heat the olive oil in a large skillet over medium heat. When the oil is hot, fry the artichokes for 12 minutes on each side, until crisp and tender. The artichokes are done when you can pull the leaves out with little resistance. Drain them on paper towels or napkins, remove to a warm platter, and serve immediately.

Grilled Vegetable Pizza with Fontina

I've updated this traditional recipe by using fontina cheese. You can have a lot of fun with this pizza by substituting different kinds of vegetables. As with all pizzas, it's great for lunch, as a snack or treat for the kids, as an appetizer before a multi-course meal, or as an accompaniment to Monday Night Football.

Makes 2 individual pizzas

½ recipe pizza dough (see Basic Recipes, page 217)

Sauce

1 pound very ripe plum tomatoes

salt

¼ cup tomato puree

8 fresh basil leaves, julienned

2 tablespoons olive oil

Topping

¼ cup extra virgin olive oil

2 cloves garlic, chopped

juice of 1 lemon

1 small eggplant, peeled and cut into circles ¼-inch thick

1 small zucchini, sliced lengthwise ¼-inch thick

1 red onion, cut into 10 even wedges

2 small portobello mushrooms

2 tablespoons pine nuts

½ cup small cubes fontina cheese

salt and pepper to taste

Preheat the oven to 450° F. Prepare the dough as instructed in the basic recipe.

To make the sauce: Peel, seed, and dice the tomatoes. Sprinkle with salt and allow them to drain in a colander for half an hour. Then place them in a bowl with the puree, basil, and olive oil and mix well. Spoon the sauce over the formed dough.

To make the topping: Prepare a grill. Combine the olive oil, garlic, and lemon juice in a bowl. Add the sliced eggplant, sliced zucchini, onion, and mushrooms and marinate for about 2 minutes. Cook the vegetables on the grill for about 3 to 4 minutes. If you can't grill, simply sauté them in a nonstick pan with a small amount of olive oil. Slice the mushrooms and sprinkle over the pizza. Place the other vegetables on the pizza. Top with the pine nuts and cheese. Season with salt and pepper.

Bake on a cookie sheet or pizza stone until the dough is crispy, about 12 minutes. Remove from the oven, slice it with a knife and fork (you don't really need a pizza cutter), and serve immediately.

Eggplant Sauce for Pasta

This is a specialty of the region around Naples. My mother's family comes from Sant' Angela di Lombardi just outside that great city. Sant' Angela's claim to fame was that it was the site of the last big earthquake in the region.

Eggplant is a staple in my garden and, come fall, we always end up with a lot of it. As you can imagine, we've made eggplant many, many different ways over the years. This is a delicious recipe, one of the best, and easy to execute.

Serves 4 to 6 as a first course or main dish

1 large eggplant, peeled and cut into ¾-inch cubes

2 teaspoons salt

5 tablespoons extra virgin olive oil

2 cloves garlic, minced

1 onion, finely chopped

2 28-ounce cans crushed tomatoes (you can also use 3 pounds fresh tomatoes, peeled, seeded, and crushed)

1 6-ounce can tomato paste

8 fresh basil leaves, chopped

pinch of sugar

freshly ground black pepper to taste

Put the eggplant in a colander and sprinkle with the salt. Allow it to drain for 1 hour.

Heat the olive oil in a skillet over medium heat. Add the eggplant and sauté for 3 minutes, until lightly browned. Remove the eggplant and drain it on a paper towel. Cook the garlic and onion in the same pan for 4 minutes; do not burn. Add the tomatoes, tomato paste, basil, sugar, and pepper. Bring to a simmer, lower the heat, and cook, uncovered, for 15 minutes. Add the eggplant and simmer for another 15 minutes.

Fried Stuffed Zucchini Flowers

I had an Uncle Joe who had a summer house with a wonderful garden in the Catskill Mountains. The zucchini flowers from his garden were always a big treat for us kids—as long as the deer didn't get them first.

Zucchini flowers are a delicacy available in produce markets only in early summer. They cannot be kept fresh in the refrigerator for more than two to three days, so when you do come across them, buy them and use them quickly. These fried flowers are a great addition to an antipasto plate.

Serves 4 as an appetizer or side dish

16 zucchini flowers

2 tomatoes

¾ cup flour

3 eggs

¼ cup milk

salt and pepper to taste

8 ounces mozzarella cheese, shredded

¼ cup capers, rinsed and dried

1 tablespoon chopped fresh basil

2 cups olive oil

Preheat the oven to 200° F.

Wash the zucchini flowers, drain on paper towels, and reserve.

Oven-dry the tomatoes by removing the skin, slicing them in half lengthwise, and removing the seeds. Place them on a cookie sheet and bake until dry, about 45 minutes. Cool completely and dice.

Combine the flour, eggs, and milk in a large bowl. Whisk well until you have a smooth batter. Season with salt and pepper.

In a separate bowl, combine the cheese, capers, diced oven-dried tomatoes, and basil. Spoon the filling into the zucchini flowers.

Heat the oil in a large sauté pan over medium-high heat.

Gently dip the filled flowers in the batter and fry until golden brown. Drain them on paper towels and serve hot.

Escarole and Beans

This is a typical peasant dish—inexpensive, easy to make, and very delicious. It's an old Italian staple that goes equally well with fish or roasted meat main dishes. It's also excellent reheated the next day and even better the day after that.

Serves 4 as a side dish

1 cup chicken stock (see Basic Recipes, page 216)

1 large head of escarole, washed well and cut into 1-inch pieces

3 tablespoons olive oil

2 cloves garlic, finely chopped

1 16-ounce can cannellini beans

6 basil leaves, julienned

pinch of crushed red pepper flakes

½ cup grated Parmesan cheese

Place the escarole and chicken stock in a large saucepan over medium heat, bring to a boil, and simmer for one hour.

Heat the olive oil in a saucepan over medium heat and gently brown the garlic. Add the beans with their liquid. Bring to a boil for about 4 minutes. Add the bean mixture to the escarole; add the basil and let simmer for about 20 minutes. Stir occasionally with a spoon. It should have a soupy consistency. Finish the dish by adding the pepper flakes. Ladle into bowls and serve with a good Italian bread and the Parmesan cheese sprinkled on top.

Mucilli

STUFFED ESCAROLE LEAVES

In Italian—in the Neapolitan dialect of my mother's family, that is—a *mucillo* is a small, scraggly kitten. When you stuff the escarole leaves, their ribs stick out just like a kitten's, which I suppose, is how this dish got its name. This is a great vegetable recipe on its own as an appetizer or alongside a poultry or fish main dish.

Serves 10 as an appetizer or side dish, 5 as a main dish

10 large escarole leaves, washed

$\frac{1}{3}$ cup extra virgin olive oil

2 cloves garlic

2 cups fresh breadcrumbs

12 Gaeta olives, pitted and chopped

$3\frac{1}{2}$ tablespoons capers

$3\frac{1}{2}$ tablespoons white raisins

3 anchovy fillets, rinsed and chopped

$3\frac{1}{2}$ tablespoons pine nuts, toasted and chopped

$1\frac{1}{2}$ teaspoons chopped fresh Italian parsley

salt and pepper to taste

Preheat the oven to 325° F.

Blanch the escarole in a pot of salted boiling water for 1 minute. Refresh in a bowl of ice water. Remove the leaves from the water and reserve.

Heat 1 tablespoon of the olive oil in a large sauté pan over medium heat. Add the garlic and sauté until golden brown. Discard the garlic. Add the breadcrumbs to the oil. Cook the breadcrumbs slowly for 3 minutes until golden brown. Remove the pan from the heat and add 2 tablespoons of water.

Add the olives, capers, raisins, anchovies, pine nuts, and parsley. Mix well and season with salt and pepper.

Heat 2 tablespoons of the remaining olive oil and place it in a casserole dish.

Spread out the escarole leaves and spoon some of the mixture onto the center of each leaf. Roll the leaves and place them seam side down in the casserole dish. Spoon the remaining oil on top of the rolled leaves and cover. Bake for 20 minutes. Remove to a warm platter and serve hot.

Fusilli with Radicchio

Here is an excellent example of a pasta dish that can be the centerpiece of a light meal, preceded by an appetizer and/or followed by a salad. This type of dish is quick and simple to prepare and *so* delicious. The key is fresh ingredients. The pasta should be served al dente and piping hot.

Serves 4 to 6 as a first course or main dish

1 pound fusilli

3 heads radicchio

3 tablespoons olive oil

6 ounces bacon, cut into cubes

1½ teaspoons crushed red pepper flakes

1 teaspoon salt

pinch of pepper

1½ tablespoons butter, softened

3 tablespoons grated Parmesan cheese

Cook the pasta as instructed on the package.

Cut the cores out of the radicchio. Remove the leaves and cut out the large, tough white center. Place 2 to 3 leaves at a time on top of each other. Roll them into a cigar shape. Cut into julienne strips.

Heat the olive oil in a large sauté pan over medium heat. Add the bacon and cook until it is very crisp. Remove and reserve. Add the pepper flakes to the same pan and cook for 1 minute. Add the radicchio and sauté for 1 minute. Season with the salt and pepper. Combine the radicchio with the pasta, add the bacon, and toss with the butter. Sprinkle with the cheese and serve immediately.

Stuffed Zucchini

Most self-respecting Italian-American cooks have a recipe for stuffed zucchini. It's a dish that's often hard to categorize, however. Is it an appetizer? A side dish? Can it function as a main course? This version, with veal, is a little heartier than most and can definitely be served as an entrée, but it can also function as a side dish or appetizer for a multicourse feast.

Serves 8 as an appetizer or side dish, 4 as a main dish

4 medium zucchini (approximately 5 ounces each), rinsed and sliced in half, lengthwise

2 tablespoons extra virgin olive oil

¼ cup finely chopped onion

3 cloves garlic, finely chopped

¼ cup finely chopped mushrooms

¼ cup finely chopped celery

2 tablespoons dry white wine

1 pound lean veal, coarsely ground

3 tablespoons chopped fresh basil

1 teaspoon chopped fresh rosemary

¾ cup grated Parmesan cheese

1 egg, beaten

2 tablespoons butter, softened

2 teaspoons salt

2 teaspoons pepper

Preheat the oven to 375° F.

Scoop out the insides of the zucchini halves with a small spoon. Reserve the cored halves and the insides.

Heat the oil in a large sauté pan over medium heat and sauté the onion until translucent. Add the garlic and sauté for 1 to 2 minutes. Then add the mushrooms and sauté for 2 minutes more. Add the celery and the reserved insides of the zucchini and continue to cook for 2 to 3 minutes. Add the white wine and cook it down for 1 minute. Add the veal and cook, stirring occasionally with a wooden spoon, until it browns nicely, approximately 8 minutes. Stir in the basil and the rosemary and cook for 1 to 2 minutes more. Remove from the heat, place in a bowl, and allow to cool.

Once the mixture has cooled, blend in the cheese, egg, butter, salt, and pepper. Fill the cored zucchini with the mixture.

Fill a baking pan with ¼ inch of water. Place the filled zucchini halves in the pan and bake for 40 minutes, until golden brown. Remove the zucchini carefully from the pan to a warm platter, spooning the juices from the pan on top of them, and serve.

Inzimino of Ceci Beans with Swiss Chard

Whenever there's an abundance of anything, Italian-Americans will find 50 ways to cook it. This recipe is great because you can substitute a lot of different vegetables. If you don't want to use Swiss chard you can use dandelion greens, kale, or any other similar green.

Inzimino is an almost impossible word to translate, but call this a stew or a soup if you like or, if you're in a musical frame of mind, a "duet" of ceci beans and Swiss chard.

If you're starting with dried beans, they need to be soaked overnight. Canned chickpeas can be substituted. If you're using the canned chickpeas, omit the first two steps.

Serves 6 as a side dish or for lunch

1 cup dried ceci beans (chickpeas, garbanzos)
1 clove garlic
7 tablespoons olive oil
2 pounds Swiss chard, stemmed
1 red onion, chopped

2 carrots, peeled and finely diced

salt and pepper to taste

pinch of crushed red pepper flakes

1 cup white wine

2 tablespoons tomato paste

1 cup chicken stock (see Basic Recipes, page 216)

12 sprigs fresh Italian parsley, stemmed and
  chopped

2 tablespoons lemon juice

Soak the beans in cold water to cover overnight.

Drain the beans and place them in a large pot
with 3 quarts of cold water, the garlic, and
2 tablespoons of the olive oil. Place over medium
heat and simmer for 45 minutes, until the beans
are tender. Drain and remove the garlic clove and
set the beans aside in a bowl.

Wash the Swiss chard and blanch in salted
boiling water for 3 minutes, drain and refresh in
ice water. Squeeze out the excess water and
coarsely chop the Swiss chard.

Heat the remaining 5 tablespoons of olive oil in
a frying pan over medium heat. Add the onion
and carrots and sauté for 4 to 5 minutes. Add
the pepper flakes and wine and cook for 4 to
5 minutes until wine is evaporated. Add the Swiss
chard and the beans, mix well, and season with
salt and pepper to taste.

Dissolve the tomato paste in the chicken stock
and add to the beans and Swiss chard mixture.
Cook for 8 to 10 minutes. Sprinkle with the
parsley, add the lemon juice, spoon into bowls,
and serve immediately. This dish goes very well
with a good crusty Italian bread.

Pasta, Ricotta, and Dandelion Pie

Springtime means dandelion greens, picked young
so they are tender and not too bitter. It was a family tradition to send the kids out to scour the
lawns for these succulent greens. Since they are
so plentiful, the recipes are endless. This is one of
my favorites. You don't have to go combing your
neighbors' lawns if you don't want to; dandelion
greens are readily available in markets in the
spring. Look for small leaves that don't have any
yellow in them.

Serves 6 as an appetizer, first course, or for lunch

Pasta

$1/2$ cup water

$1/4$ cup extra virgin olive oil

$1/4$ teaspoon salt

$3 1/4$ cups flour, approximately

Filling

2 tablespoons extra virgin olive oil

$1/2$ onion, peeled and finely chopped

1 clove garlic, peeled and finely chopped

7 cups dandelion greens, tough stems removed,
  washed well

14 ounces whole-milk ricotta cheese

2 eggs

1 teaspoon chopped fresh marjoram

1 teaspoon salt

freshly ground white pepper

1 cup grated parmesan cheese

To make the pasta: Combine the water and olive oil in a bowl. Gradually stir in the salt and enough flour to form a soft, pliable dough. Turn the dough out onto a floured board and knead until smooth, about 2 minutes. Cover with a damp towel and let rest for 1 hour.

To make the filling: Heat 1 teaspoon of the olive oil in a skillet over medium heat. Add the onion and garlic and cook for 2 minutes. Add the dandelion greens and cook for 3 minutes more. Allow to cool. In a bowl, whisk together the ricotta, eggs, marjoram, salt, and pepper. Coarsely chop the dandelion greens and combine them well with the mixture.

Divide the pasta dough into 4 pieces, with 2 pieces slightly larger than the other 2. On a lightly floured surface, roll out the large pieces into rectangles about 12 x 8 inches and the small ones into rectangles about 11 x 6 inches, keeping the unused portions in a damp towel while you work.

Preheat the oven to 350° F.

Brush an $11^3/_4$ x $7^1/_2$ x $1^3/_4$-inch baking dish or pan with 1 teaspoon of olive oil. Place one of the larger rectangles in the bottom of the dish and brush with 1 teaspoon of olive oil. Spread a third of the filling over the dough, leaving a $^3/_4$-inch border. Sprinkle on $^1/_4$ cup of the Parmesan cheese. Top with one of the smaller rectangles, brush with 1 teaspoon of olive oil. Spread half of the remaining filling over it and sprinkle with $^1/_4$ cup Parmesan. Top with the remaining small pasta sheet and brush with 1 teaspoon of olive oil. Spread the remaining filling over it and sprinkle with $^1/_4$ cup Parmesan. Top with the remaining large sheet of pasta and press the bottom sheet and the top sheets together, folding them over to form a rim. Brush with the remaining teaspoon of olive oil.

Bake for 45 minutes, then cover with aluminum foil and continue baking until the pasta is tender throughout, about 15 minutes longer. Preheat the broiler. Uncover the dish and sprinkle with the remaining $^1/_4$ cup of Parmesan. Broil until the cheese is browned, about 1 minute. Cut into squares and serve.

Neapolitan Stuffed Peppers

Every family has a stuffed pepper recipe. I think that this one, as simple as it is, ranks with the greatest. It's a showcase for good fresh ingredients, made in the time-honored way with lots of love and pride. These stuffed peppers are very good as leftovers, refrigerated and reheated.

Serves 6 as a side dish

6 red peppers

2 tablespoons white raisins

$1/2$ cup olive oil, plus more as needed

1 cup breadcrumbs

30 black olives, pitted and quartered

7 anchovy fillets, rinsed and chopped

1 bunch fresh Italian parsley, chopped

1 bunch fresh basil, chopped

2 tablespoons grated Parmesan cheese

3 tablespoons capers, rinsed

1 recipe Garden Tomato Sauce (see Basic Recipes, page 217)

Cut the tops off the peppers and clean out the seeds. Reserve.

Soak the raisins in water for 10 minutes, then drain and reserve.

Preheat the oven to 325° F.

Heat the olive oil in a large sauté pan over medium heat. Add the breadcrumbs and cook, stirring constantly, until toasted. Lower the heat and add the raisins, olives, anchovies, parsley, basil, cheese, and capers. (If the mixture is too dry, add a little more oil.)

Brush a small lasagna pan with a little olive oil. Fill the peppers with the breadcrumb mixture and arrange them in an upright position in the pan. If they don't stand well, carefully slice across the bottoms with a paring knife to level them off, being careful not to remove too much.

Spoon some tomato sauce on top and bake for 35 minutes or until the peppers are tender. Remove carefully to warm plates, spoon more sauce on top, and serve hot.

Pasta with Wild Greens and Ricotta

This is a very popular Southern Italian dish. We use many different types of greens, depending on the season. You can substitute broccoli rabe, Swiss chard, escarole, kale, collard greens, mustard greens, dandelion greens, or even a combination. Traditionally, this recipe calls for a piece of ricotta salata on top. Salata is a ricotta that has been drained of excess liquid and slightly aged. This may not be readily available, so in this version I substituted fresh ricotta cheese.

Serves 4 to 6 as a first course or for lunch

2¼ **pounds greens (broccoli rabe, Swiss chard, escarole, kale, collard greens, mustard greens, dandelion greens, or a combination)**

¼ **cup extra virgin olive oil**

1 **clove garlic, minced**

salt to taste

crushed red pepper flakes to taste

1 **pound bucatini or perciatelli pasta**

¼ **pound ricotta cheese**

½ **cup grated pecorino cheese**

Wash the greens very well. Cook them in lightly salted water, uncovered, for 8 to 10 minutes. Remove from the water and chop them coarsely. Reserve the cooking water.

Heat the olive oil over medium heat in a sauté pan. Add the garlic and greens and sauté for 3 to 4 minutes. Season with salt and pepper flakes, then remove from the heat.

Bring the water from the greens back to a boil and use it to cook the pasta as instructed on the package. Drain and reserve ¾ cup of the liquid. Toss the pasta with half the greens and the reserved liquid. Spoon the remaining greens on top of that, spoon the ricotta cheese on top, sprinkle with pecorino cheese, and serve.

Torta di Verdura

VEGETABLE TART

This delicious vegetable tart goes very well with a nice salad of arugula. If you have some extra vegetables on hand, this dish is the perfect way to put them to use.

Serves 6 as an appetizer, first course, or for lunch

Crust

3 extra-large eggs

¼ cup sugar

1 teaspoon grated lemon zest

10 tablespoons butter, at room temperature

¾ cup flour

pinch of salt

1 teaspoon baking powder

Filling

3 tablespoons butter

1 tablespoon olive oil

**2 pounds Swiss chard, cleaned, stemmed, and cut
    into 1-inch strips**

6 slices stale white bread, crusts removed

1 cup milk

2 extra-large eggs

⅓ cup grated Parmesan cheese

3 tablespoons white raisins

2½ tablespoons pine nuts

pinch of grated nutmeg

3 tablespoons sugar

pinch of salt

¼ cup brandy

To make the crust: Place the eggs, sugar, and lemon zest in a bowl, and mix well. Add the butter and mix very well. Place the flour in a mound on a clean surface. Make a well in the center and place the butter mixture in the well. Add the salt and mix the flour into the butter mixture to form a ball of dough. Add the baking powder and knead the dough for 1 more minute. Wrap in plastic wrap and refrigerate for 1 to 2 hours.

To make the filling: Heat the butter and olive oil in a frying pan over medium heat. Add the Swiss chard and sauté for 8 to 10 minutes until wilted. Set aside in a bowl.

Soak the bread in the milk for 15 minutes. Remove the bread, squeezing out the excess milk. Add the bread to the Swiss chard. Add the eggs, cheese, raisins, pine nuts, nutmeg, sugar, salt, and brandy. Mix well.

Preheat the oven to 375° F. Lightly butter a round 10 x 1-inch tart mold, preferably with a removable bottom.

Roll out the dough into a circle 16 inches in diameter and ¼ inch thick. Place the dough in the tart pan, pressing it down into the mold. Roll the rolling pin over the top of the rim of the tart mold to cut off the excess dough. Place the filling in the shell and bake for 1 hour, until golden brown. Remove from the oven and allow to rest for 10 minutes. Cut into wedges and serve warm.

Sicilian Roasted Pepper Salad

This is one of my staple dishes in the summer, especially if I'm throwing a party. It is fast and simple but should be prepared and dressed at least one hour ahead. It's red, green, and white, the colors of the Italian flag, which adds a festive look to the presentation. To roast and peel the peppers see page 224.

Serves 5 as an appetizer

**4 green peppers, roasted, peeled, and cut into
   ¼-inch strips**

**4 red peppers, roasted, peeled, and cut into
   ¼-inch strips**

¾ pound fresh mozzarella cheese, thinly sliced

1 anchovy fillet, finely chopped

1 egg yolk

2 tablespoons red wine vinegar

1 cup extra virgin olive oil

½ red onion, finely chopped

⅛ teaspoon crushed red pepper flakes

2 tablespoons chopped fresh Italian parsley

2 tablespoons capers, rinsed and chopped

⅛ teaspoon salt

Arrange the peppers and cheese on a serving platter. In a mixing bowl, place the anchovy, egg yolk, and vinegar. Begin to whisk and start to drizzle the olive oil into the bowl. When you have completely incorporated all the oil, add the onion, pepper flakes, parsley, capers, and salt. Drizzle the dressing over the peppers and cheese. Serve at room temperature. Cover the leftovers and store in the refrigerator for up to 3 days.

Colavita Extra Virgin Olive Oil

A Pipeline from the Old Country

Among the many fascinating and quirky traditions Italian-Americans keep alive is the little-known practice of eating lentil soup on New Year's Eve at midnight while walking up and down the stairs. You've never heard of that one? Neither had John Profaci, Sr., and his family until 1978 when they witnessed it at the house of some good friends in Bay Ridge, Brooklyn. That was the same year John Sr. started his most successful business, Colavita USA, and his eldest son, Joseph R. Profaci, was accepted to Harvard College. Ever since, on New Year's Eve you will find the Profacis on the stairway with the lentil soup. They don't want to risk losing their good fortune.

John Sr. grew up in Bay Ridge, Brooklyn, started a pizza parlor in Sheepshead Bay when he graduated from college, and continued to work in the food business, eventually becoming a broker for a number of importing firms. In 1978, he was put in touch with Enrico Colavita from Molise, Italy, which is about two hours southeast of Rome. Enrico and his brother Leonardo were in charge of the family olive oil business there. For many years the Colavitas had operated a *frantoio*, an olive mill and press that serviced all the local growers. They created their own brand in the 1970s, then realized that the only way to expand was to go abroad.

"In those days, outside of food professionals, extra virgin olive oil was virtually unknown in this country," Joseph R. says. "So the timing was perfect."

John Sr. met with Enrico Colavita and agreed to a trip to Italy—his first ever—to check out the facility. When he got there, he liked what he saw and they worked out an arrangement for the founding of Colavita USA, the exclusive importer of Colavita products.

John Sr., both of whose parents came from Sicily, employs all four of his sons, Joseph R., John Jr., Robert, and Anthony, in the business. In addition, John Sr.'s brother Joe works there.

Colavita extra virgin olive oil, with its rich, almost buttery flavor, at first was sold only in food-service outlets for restaurants and through the ethnic specialty distributors. At the top of its category in just about every measure, it's now available in most retail outlets nationwide. Colavita's product line has since expanded to include pasta sauces, vinegar, and recently the Ferrara line of food products (from the famous Ferrara Café in Manhattan's Little Italy).

What qualifies as "extra virgin olive oil"? It is the highest grade, the best you can buy. The olives are harvested by hand. The trees are either beaten with sticks or the olives are plucked off them so they collect in nets or burlap sacks placed around the foot of the trees. Then they are taken to the *frantoio* where they are mashed into a paste, pits and all. The paste is then spread on mats, which are stacked and pressed together by a machine press. Out seeps the olive oil. It's allowed to settle and any excess water is removed, either by centrifuge or decanting. It is pure, unrefined and unprocessed, which is why they call it virgin. Some extra virgin oil is filtered to remove the tiny microscopic pieces of solid material in it. This does not affect the taste or quality in any way. The only difference is the unfiltered oil might be a little cloudy until it settles.

To qualify as extra virgin, the oil must have less than 1% free oleic acid, which is the primary fatty chemical in olive oil. Any damage or defect to the olives or the oil, such as bruising or fermentation, jars loose a molecule in the chain of this precious substance, setting it free. This in turn affects the oil, giving it an "off taste" or slight rancidity that is hard to describe but is comparable to the flavor of an over-ripe pumpkin.

Top-quality extra virgin olive oil like Colavita costs a little more, but its advantages in terms of taste and health over other oils and fats are more than worth the extra expense. Connoisseurs usually categorize the flavor of fine olive oils as mild, semi-fruity, and fruity. Many of the finer brands from Tuscany and Southern Italy have a peppery finish.

Olive oil is one of the most important ingredients in our Little Italy cuisine. Not only does it enhance just about every recipe, it's also great with a little red wine vinegar, salt, and pepper as a salad dressing, or served plain in a dish for dipping a good piece of bread in.

One tablespoon of olive oil contains 120 calories, 14 grams of fat and no cholesterol; it is 77% monounsaturated fat, 9% polyunsaturated fat, and 14% vegetable derived saturated fat. Compare this to a tablespoon of butter, which contains 8 grams of saturated fat (66%) and 33 milligrams of cholesterol. Olive oil delivers the most monounsaturated fats (that's the good kind) of any vegetable oil. Yes, it's high in calories, but they are good calories.

Olive oil is produced in all the countries bordering the Mediterranean Sea: France, Greece, Israel, Italy, Morocco, Portugal, Spain, Tunisia, and Turkey. It's even produced in California, because the Spanish monks who founded that state many years ago brought it from their native land. But, in my opinion, the best olive oil comes from Italy, and the best of the best is Colavita.

A final and important note on storage: Olive oil should be kept in a cool, dark place—definitely not in the refrigerator, where it can solidify and crystalize. The oil can keep for up to two years, but its peak is for the first year, and it's most flavorful for the first two months.

Chapter Five

La caccia

La caccia means the hunt. In the fall, it's not just about the men **hunting** for game,
it's about the whole family going out mushroom-picking in the woods or pressing grapes at home.
It's about the hearty dishes, the stews and soups, that taste just right when you come in from the
cold. The recipes in this chapter are all inspired by the rituals and traditions of the fall and the hunt.

Our family keeps the mushroom-picking tradition going. My father and uncles know which **mushrooms** to pick and they've passed the knowledge down to my generation. We pick what we call the *mammi funghi*, the "mother of mushrooms," a large wild mushroom that usually grows near the base of oak **trees** and is quite prevalent in the Northeast. In upstate New York, you can also find chanterelles growing wild, as well as the occasional morel, another special treat.

If she doesn't go along, my **grandmother** is always ready to check out the mushrooms we bring back. She keeps an old silver quarter that she throws into the pan where the mushrooms are **cooking**. If the coin turns dark, she throws the mushrooms away. Scientists might argue with that test, but she's been picking mushrooms for most of her 80 years, and she hasn't poisoned anybody yet.

Italians, including my grandfather, would make their own wine in the fall. At the end of September, the grapes would come in from California to the **Brooklyn** Terminal Market. If you didn't grow them in your backyard you could buy them by the case and press them at home. It was a great asset to have our own wine to give as a gift for the holidays—and to sip with **meals** all year round.

In Southern Italy, where my family comes from, hunting was mostly just for the rich. My father came to this country poor, and to him hunting was a luxury. As soon as he made a few dollars, he began going hunting with his brothers in the fall, and this became another cherished family tradi-

tion. After the hunt, the men would all cook, sit down around the table for a meal and a glass of **wine**, then spend the evening playing cards and telling stories. As soon as I was old enough to join them, I found out that the best card games and the best storytelling went on around that table, not to mention some of the best cooking. It was a classic male **ritual**.

One of my father's favorite hunting stories is of when he first came from Italy and wanted to go hunting. He didn't have enough money to go too far upstate, but in those days you didn't have to. All he wanted to hunt was rabbit, but he figured he needed a dog. He found another guy from Sicily who seemed to know something about hunting, and he offered to sell my father a beagle for $20. He said the dog was already trained to hunt rabbits. My father was shocked. "For $20 this dog can hunt rabbits?" The guy said, "Definitely. I'm doing this as a favor to you, a fellow Sicilian." So my father bought the dog and took him hunting. When a rabbit came running out of his hole the dog started chasing it. My father said to himself, "This dog is good. For $20, it's unbelievable how well he hunts." The dog flushed the rabbit, my father aimed his gun, fired a shot, and bagged the rabbit. Then he looked for his dog. He was gone. For $20, my father got a dog that was gun-shy. One shot and the dog ran away, never to be seen again! To this day, he won't talk to that guy who sold him a lousy dog for $20. My father went on to have plenty of good hunting dogs, German shorthairs, and in fact he made sure they knew what they were doing because he bred and trained them himself.

Anthony and Paul learn the art of storytelling.

Wild Duck with Lentils

As soon as I was old enough to walk, my father began taking me duck hunting. On cold January mornings, we would hunt ducks by the ocean on Long Island or the Chesapeake Bay. These were wonderful trips, always punctuated by cold evenings where we would sample our game around a warm fire. Here is a recipe that brings back all those good memories for me.

Serves 4 as a main course

1 medium wild duck, cleaned

salt and pepper

2 tablespoons olive oil

3 slices bacon, chopped

1 clove garlic

1 small white onion, sliced

1½ tablespoons flour

1 bay leaf

1 stalk celery, finely diced

1 carrot, peeled and diced

1 cup button mushrooms, washed and cut in half

½ cup white wine

4 cups chicken stock (see Basic Recipes, page 216)

2 cups cooked lentils

1 tablespoon chopped fresh Italian parsley

Start by cutting the duck into 8 pieces, the same way you would cut a chicken. Season well with salt and pepper.

Heat the olive oil in a heavy casserole over medium heat. Add the duck and sauté, skin side down, until well-browned. Turn the duck over and spoon off the excess fat. Add the bacon, garlic, and onion and allow to cook for 3 to 4 minutes. Then sprinkle with the flour and sauté for another 2 to 3 minutes. (The flour will act as a thickening agent for your sauce.) Add the bay leaf, celery, carrot, and mushrooms and stir. Cook for 4 minutes, then add the wine and cook until it evaporates. Add the chicken stock, allow it to come to a boil, and reduce the heat to low. Cover the casserole and simmer very gently for 40 minutes.

Reheat the lentils if necessary and place on a warm platter. Skim any excess fat off the top of the casserole broth with a spoon, sprinkle with the parsley, season with salt and pepper to taste, spoon the duck and sauce on top of the lentils, and serve immediately.

Scrambled Eggs with Mushrooms and Pancetta

When my family picks mushrooms we always end up with many more than we know what to do with. This recipe is an excellent solution to that *abbondanza*. It's good for breakfast, brunch, or a late-night snack.

Serves 4 for breakfast, lunch, or snack

2 tablespoons olive oil

¼ pound pancetta, cut into small dice

¼ cup pine nuts

1 small onion, chopped

1 clove garlic, chopped

1 pound mixed mushrooms, cleaned and sliced

1 teaspoon salt

pepper to taste

¼ cup white wine

¼ cup chopped fresh Italian parsley

6 eggs, slightly beaten

1 tablespoon chopped fresh chives

Heat the olive oil in a medium-size sauté pan over medium heat. Add the pancetta and sauté until crispy. Remove the pancetta from the pan and place in a bowl. Leave the remaining oil and fat in the pan.

Add the pine nuts to the pan and sauté them until they have a nice golden color. Remove them from the pan with a slotted spoon. Combine the pine nuts with the cooked pancetta in the bowl. Again, reserve the oil and fat.

Cook the onion in the pan over medium heat until translucent, approximately 4 to 5 minutes. Add the garlic and cook for 1 to 2 minutes more. Add the mushrooms, salt, and pepper and sauté for 3 to 4 minutes. Add the wine and cook until reduced by half. Toss the pancetta and pine nuts back into the pan with the mushroom mixture. Stir in the parsley. Remove from the heat.

Separately season and scramble the eggs, then cook in a clean sauté pan. Place on warm plates, spoon the mushroom mixture over the top, sprinkle with the chives, and serve immediately.

Polenta with a Ragu of Wild Mushrooms

Ragu is a traditional hearty Italian stew-type sauce, the classic version being the Bolognese meat and tomato sauce for pasta. My family would always make this type of recipe with soft polenta, but I've jazzed it up a bit by cooling the polenta, cutting it into triangles, and searing it in a little olive oil.

Serves 4 as a first course

3 tablespoons extra virgin olive oil

1 cup polenta

½ cup grated Parmesan cheese

2 shallots, chopped

1 small clove garlic, diced

2 cups mixed wild mushrooms, picked clean and lightly washed

1 small tomato, peeled, seeded, and diced

4 fresh basil leaves, julienned

salt and white pepper to taste

fresh basil sprig for garnish

Place 1 quart of boiling salted water and 1 tablespoon of the olive oil in a pot over medium heat. Bring to a boil for 2 minutes. Remove the pan from the heat and quickly pour the polenta into the water, beating with a wooden spoon. Return the pan to the heat and continue cooking for 5 to 6 minutes over medium heat, stirring constantly. Turn off the heat and add the cheese, mixing well. Turn the polenta out into a nonstick 11 x 17-inch lasagna pan and allow to cool and harden. (It helps to chill it for a while in the fridge.) Remove the polenta from the pan and cut into small triangles.

Heat 1 tablespoon of olive oil in a small saucepan over medium heat. Add the shallots and cook until translucent, then add the garlic and mushrooms. Cook for 3 minutes. Add the tomato and basil and set aside for 2 minutes.

Lightly brush the polenta triangles with 1½ teaspoons of olive oil and sear in a nonstick skillet over medium heat until golden brown and crispy. Repeat on the other side.

Spoon the mushrooms in the middle of a warm platter and arrange the polenta on top. Garnish with a sprig of basil and serve.

Polenta with Sausage and Tomato Sauce

This is one of those stick-to-your-ribs dishes that's perfect when you've been out in the cold too long and your hands are so numb you can't move your fingers. Not only is this dish going to warm your body, it's going to warm your heart.

Serves 4 to 6 as a first course or main dish

1 tablespoon olive oil

1 pound sweet Italian sausage, cut into 2-inch pieces

½ pound cremini mushrooms

1 recipe Garden Tomato Sauce (see Basic Recipes, page 217)

1 cup instant polenta

2 tablespoons butter

3 tablespoons mascarpone cheese

¼ cup grated Parmesan cheese

2 teaspoons salt

pinch of pepper

Heat the olive oil in a large sauté pan and cook the sausage over medium heat. Add the mushrooms, and continue to sauté for another 3 to 4 minutes. Mix with the tomato sauce and reserve.

Prepare the polenta as instructed on the package. Immediately after the final stage of cooking, stir in the butter and cheeses, and season with the salt and pepper. Spoon the polenta onto individual plates or a platter, making a well for the sauce. Spoon the sauce into the well and serve immediately.

Paparadelle al Cacciatore

PASTA "HUNTER STYLE"

You've heard of chicken *cacciatore*, a very popular dish. Well, here's another *cacciatore*, with a hearty sauce blending the flavors of four types of meats, including rabbit.

Paparadelle are a very wide and fairly thick noodle; they add a rustic touch to this dish. If they're not available, you could use another type of noodle. For an extra treat, serve this dish with a spoonful of ricotta cheese on top. Delicious!

Serves 4 to 6 as a first course or main dish

3 tablespoons extra virgin olive oil

meat of 2 small chickens, thighs and legs removed from the bone and cut into ¼-inch dice

meat of 2 rabbit legs, removed from the bone and cut into ¼-inch dice

6 ounces pork shoulder, minced

1 sweet Italian sausage, casing removed, minced

3 garlic cloves, finely minced

1 white onion, finely chopped

¼ cup chopped fresh Italian parsley

½ cup dry red wine

3 cups Garden Tomato Sauce (see Basic Recipes, page 217)

salt and freshly ground black pepper to taste

1 pound paparadelle noodles (preferably fresh)

grated Parmesan or pecorino cheese for garnish

Heat the olive oil in a deep skillet over medium heat. Add all the meats and lightly brown them, about 3 to 4 minutes. Remove the meat with a slotted spoon and drain on paper towels. Pour all but 2 tablespoons of fat from the pan. Add the garlic, onion, and parsley and cook on low heat for 3 minutes. Return the meat to the skillet, add the wine, and cook until the wine is reduced by half. Add the tomato sauce, salt, and pepper. Cook for 10 minutes over medium heat.

Cook the paparadelle in boiling salted water, drain, and serve with the sauce on top and a sprinkle of grated cheese if you like.

Cleaning Mushrooms

When picking mushrooms, always look for the ones that are tightly closed and firm. They should be very white and dry. When cleaning mushrooms, if they are not very dirty, simply brush them off with a small brush. If they are caked with a fair amount of dirt, brush them off and quickly wash with cold water, then pat dry. Be careful they don't absorb too much water and become soggy.

Grilled Squab

As a kid, I can remember being shocked that I was the butt of jokes at school when I said we had had pigeon for dinner the night before. I didn't see what the big deal was. Pigeon is delicious. What a pity that a lot of people just won't try dishes like rabbit or pigeon because they have certain ideas in their heads about those animals. The pigeon you eat is *not* the pigeon you see in the park, which I guess is why we prefer to call it squab. They are savory, meaty little birds, and this is a great recipe with which to discover the pleasure of eating them.

Serves 4 as a main course

4 medium squabs, split in half

¼ cup olive oil

salt and pepper

**2 tablespoons plus 1 teaspoon mustard
(preferably a strong type such as Dijon)**

1 cup breadcrumbs

1 teaspoon butter

1 teaspoon flour

½ cup red wine vinegar

5 black peppercorns, cracked

⅛ teaspoon crushed red pepper flakes

1 cup chicken stock (see Basic Recipes, page 216)

½ teaspoon tomato paste

1 tablespoon capers, chopped

Prepare a grill or broiler.

Brush the squabs with some of the olive oil, then sprinkle with salt and pepper. Grill or broil for 8 minutes per side. When they are nearly done, brush the squabs with 4 teaspoons of the mustard and sprinkle with the breadcrumbs. Brush the squabs lightly with olive oil again and allow to cook for 3 more minutes, until lightly browned. To test the squabs for doneness, poke a toothpick or small skewer into the leg joint (between the drumstick and shoulder); if there is no blood and the juices run clear, it is done. While the squabs are grilling, make the sauce. (When the squabs are done, remove to a warm platter while they await the sauce.)

Melt the butter in a saucepan over medium heat. When it begins to sizzle, sprinkle with the flour. Allow to cook for 2 to 3 minutes, add the vinegar, peppercorns, and pepper flakes. Cook for 2 minutes, then add the chicken stock and tomato paste. Stir well, lower the heat, and cook for 10 minutes. Remove from the heat, add the remaining tablespoon of mustard and the capers. Spoon the sauce over the squabs and serve immediately.

Chestnut and Fruit Fritters

Joe Cirillo, my stepmother's father, was one of the most incredible cooks I have ever met. It never ceased to amaze me how we would come in from a long day of hunting in the Catskill Mountain and he would have a great meal ready in what seemed like minutes. Many of our dinners ended next to a fire with these tasty fritters. Joe is gone now, and this, to the best of my recollection, is his recipe.

Serves 4 as a dessert or snack

2 medium apples, peeled, cored, and thinly sliced
1 cup Vin Santo or other dessert wine
$^1/_3$ cup granulated sugar
$^1/_2$ cup all-purpose flour
$^1/_2$ cup chestnut flour
1 egg, separated
$^3/_4$ cup dry white wine
1 tablespoon unsalted butter, softened
vegetable oil for frying
confectioners' sugar for dusting the fritters

Place the apple slices in a bowl and sprinkle with the Vin Santo and the granulated sugar. Cover and set aside for 1 hour.

Mix together both types of flour, the egg yolk, and the white wine. Beat the egg white in a separate bowl until fluffy. Fold the egg white gently into the flour mixture. Drain the apples and mix gently into the batter.

Heat $^1/_2$ inch of vegetable oil in a heavy skillet over medium heat. Drop a 5-inch round of batter in the skillet, cook until golden brown on one side, flip and cook likewise on the other side. This should take about 3 minutes ($1^1/_2$ minutes per side). Remove, drain, dust with the confectioners' sugar, and serve.

Pumpkin Gnocchi

My step-grandfather, Joe Cirillo, never wasted anything. He used to take the leftover pumpkins from Halloween and make these gnocchi. They are easy and you can freeze them.

Pumpkins are very popular in Italy. The Italian version is smaller, more like a gourd, but it still has that nice meaty flesh.

Serves 4 as a first course

$1^1/_2$ pounds pumpkin, peeled, seeded, and cut into 2-inch cubes
$^1/_4$ cup plus 3 tablespoons unsalted butter, melted
$^3/_4$ cup grated Parmesan cheese

½ teaspoon ground mace

salt and pepper to taste

3 egg yolks, beaten

1 cup flour

Preheat the oven to 325° F.

Toss the pumpkin with ¼ cup of the melted butter. Place in a baking pan and bake for about 30 minutes, until tender. Mash the pumpkin with a potato masher or pass it through a food mill. Mix with ½ cup of the cheese, the mace, and season with salt and pepper. Add the egg yolks and flour. Knead until it forms a dough.

Divide the dough into 9 pieces. Roll each piece evenly into a long cylinder about ½-inch thick. Cut each cylinder into 1-inch long croquettes. Press each piece slightly with the prongs of a fork.

Bring 4 quarts of salted water to a rapid boil in a large pot. Place the gnocchi in the pot and cook for 3 to 5 minutes. Once boiled, drain them in a colander, then transfer to a bowl. Toss with the remaining 3 tablespoons butter and ¼ cup Parmesan and serve immediately.

Rigatoni with Mushroom Sauce

I love all kinds of mushrooms. This recipe calls for white mushrooms because I wanted to make it accessible to the widest possible audience, but you can make it with just about any kind of mushroom. The sauce also tastes great on polenta, chicken, even fish.

Serves 4 to 6 as a first course or main dish

⅓ cup olive oil

1 small onion, chopped

4 cloves garlic, chopped

1 pound white mushrooms, washed and sliced

¼ cup white wine

3 anchovy fillets, rinsed and chopped

1 pound canned Italian plum tomatoes, seeded and diced

2 tablespoons chopped fresh Italian parsley

1 pound rigatoni

½ teaspoon salt

pinch of pepper

Heat the olive oil in a large saucepan over medium heat. Add the onion and sauté until slightly translucent. Add the garlic and continue to cook the mixture until the garlic is golden in color. Add the mushrooms and sauté for 2 to 3 minutes. Add the white wine and cook until reduced by half.

Stir in the anchovies, tomatoes, and parsley and simmer the mixture for 10 minutes.

While the sauce is simmering, cook the pasta as instructed on the package.

Season the sauce with the salt and pepper, mix well with the cooked pasta, and serve immediately.

Stewed Rabbit

My Uncle Eddie has property in upstate New York where I used to hunt rabbits with my cousins. In the evening, our catch would be transformed into this wonderful dish. Rabbit is readily available at your local butcher, who can cut it up for you. Some people don't like the taste of the kidneys and liver; if you don't, simply omit them. Chicken can be substituted for the rabbit if you prefer.

Serve this dish with soft polenta, fresh pasta, or Parmesan Mashed Potatoes (page 33) on the side.

Serves 4 as a main dish

1 fryer rabbit, about 3$^{1}/_{2}$ pounds, cut into eighths and fat removed

salt and pepper

$^{1}/_{4}$ cup olive oil

$^{1}/_{4}$ pound pancetta, cut into small dice

2 onions, chopped

3 cloves garlic, smashed

2 cups cremini mushrooms, washed and cut in half; if cremini are unavailable use button mushrooms

$^{1}/_{2}$ cup dry white wine

3 pepperoncini, seeded and chopped

4 tomatoes, peeled, seeded, and diced

$^{3}/_{4}$ cup chicken stock (see Basic Recipes, page 216)

4 sprigs fresh thyme

2 sprigs fresh oregano

2 tablespoons capers, rinsed

Season the rabbit well with salt and pepper.

Heat the olive oil in a large sauté pan. Fry the rabbit pieces in the oil over medium heat until they are nicely browned. Once browned, remove the pieces from the pan and keep in a warm place. Leave the oil in the pan.

Brown the pancetta in the oil. Add the onion and cook for 4 minutes over medium heat. Add the garlic and sauté for 2 minutes. Add the mushrooms and cook for 3 minutes, then add the white wine. Cook the mixture until the wine is reduced by half. Add the pepperoncini, tomatoes, chicken stock, thyme, and oregano. Place the rabbit pieces back in the pan and continue to simmer for 15 minutes.

After 15 minutes, mix in the capers, spoon equal portions of the dish onto warm plates and serve immediately.

Iano from Vasto

Home Winemaking at Its Best

I was looking for someone who makes wine the way my grandfather used to make it, and Anna Nurse introduced me to Sebastiano La Verghetta. What a find this man is! He makes some of the best homemade wine I've ever had—in fairly large quantities. Most homemade wines have a lot of tannin. Not Iano's; it's wonderful—very tasty, very fruity. Not only are the results of his labors excellent, but the winemaking itself is an all-day ritual filled with good food and camaraderie.

Sebastiano, who is known as Iano (pronounced "Yano"), and his winemakers are as great a group of Italian-American characters as you're ever going to meet. There's Aldo La Vigna—his last name happens to mean "the vine" in Italian—with his two sons Joe and Paul; there's Benedetto Di Giglio. They miss Felice Mastropietro, who passed away recently, but his two sons Dino and Paul still come; and many more.

You can learn how to make wine at home by buying a book with all the instructions and a kit, or you can do it the way Iano did: by word of mouth and by experience. Iano has been making wine on his own since about 1980. He learned the secrets from his father-in-law, Giuseppe Farro, who used to make it at his house in Maplewood, New Jersey. He's not making wine anymore but his son, Iano's brother-in-law Andrew (Andrea), continues the legacy.

Iano makes his all-natural, organic wine in oak barrels every year in the early fall. The grapes are shipped from California to Corrado's in Paterson, New Jersey, where Iano buys them. (My grandfather used to buy the same high-quality types of grapes from California at the Brooklyn Terminal Market.) Iano will buy 72 cases to make four barrels of wine, which is 200 gallons.

"They let me know when the grapes are coming in at Corrado's," Iano says. "The first thing we do when we bring them home is let them sit in the garage for a day or two to dry off. They come shipped in a refrigerated railroad car so there's some condensation."

The next step is crushing the grapes. Iano solicits the help of a couple friends and, on a Monday or Tuesday night in late September, they feed them into the grinder. The juice and the crushed grapes go straight into open barrels where they ferment for five to seven days. This brings us to a Sunday and the ceremony of pressing the grapes. This is a big celebration. Everybody lends a hand. The grapes are pressed in the garage; meanwhile, Iano's wife Carmela singlehandedly prepares a traditional six-course feast in the kitchen not far away. The juice is siphoned off from the pressed grapes and left in open barrels for two more days to ferment. It

bubbles and Iano skims any particles or debris off the top. Next the wine-to-be goes into clean barrels, which are loosely capped to allow for some air circulation but no contamination. Any kind of foreign particle or spores that sneak in can ruin the delicate fermentation process and destroy the wine.

"Cleanliness in wine-making is very important," Iano explains. "You've got to scrape those barrels out and rinse them clean to get rid of any old sediment from previous batches. Also, you've got to get out every drop of water. The barrels have to be clean and dry before you put the wine in." It takes three people a full day to scrape and rinse out the ten barrels that Iano uses in the course of a year of wine-making.

While the red-wine grapes are allowed to ferment before pressing, grapes for the white wine are crushed and pressed on the same day because if the crushed grapes are given any time to ferment in their skins, the wine starts to take on a darker tint and Iano prefers a light-colored white wine.

The wine stays in the loosely tapped barrel for

three weeks to a month. "I put my ear to the barrel and when I hear no more bubbling in there, I know the fermentation has stopped and it's time to seal the barrels," Iano says. The wine then ages in its barrels until late December, when it's time to try it. "Traditionally I first taste the wine at Christmas. It's drinkable, it's good, but it's still young. At that point, the year-old vintage is really wine, but we don't save a lot past a full year."

In January, it's time to clean three or four barrels and siphon the current batch off into those clean barrels, or into demijohns. This cleaning and siphoning process happens every two months or so to avoid contamination or spoilage and to eliminate sediment that naturally builds up. Some of the wine is also bottled, with Iano's own homemade labels, for gift-giving or travel.

The alcohol content of Iano's wine, he figures, is about 14 to 15%, a bit higher than most store-bought wine. "Not everybody appreciates homemade wine," he says. "It's a taste you've got to get used to. But I don't drink anything else. If somebody gives me a bottle of store-bought wine, I just give it away again." He takes a little of his homemade wine when he visits his relatives back in Italy, most of whom live in Vasto or in Rome. How do they like it? "They always ask me to bring more."

In addition to all the friends, Iano's three sons help out, so this is one tradition I don't think anybody has to worry about dying out. "Sure it's hard work," Iano says, "but it's pleasant work. And then all year you get to drink some good wine."

The grapes after the pressing. Iano is in the center.

Chapter Six

La Festa

For Italian-Americans, all feasts emanate from the Roman Catholic Church. Of course, the two biggest are Christmas and Easter, followed by the saints' days that **inspire** street festivals in every Little Italy across the nation.

Christmas

In our culture, Christmas Eve is the all-important get-together for the immediate family. We eat seafood before going to midnight Mass and snack afterward. According to Italian lore, eating eel on Christmas Eve brings happiness, while eating octopus brings the promise of wealth— those eight arms can carry a lot!

Christmas Day is different, more social, less intimate. Planning and preparation for the Christmas Day feast will have been going on for weeks. Every Italian family makes twice what they can eat because it's the day everybody goes visiting. Usually, the older people stay home to receive guests while the younger generations go visiting. If you're on the visiting team, you end up going to ten different houses and eating ten different meals. You better be prepared to eat! If you're on the home team, you have to have an all-day feast ready from mid-morning until night because you never know who's going to show up at what time. In this chapter, I've included most of the typical Christmas Eve dishes along with some for Christmas Day.

Easter

Easter celebrations really start with Palm Sunday, when Italians make Easter bread, which is similar to a Jewish challah. It's a big braided loaf with colored Easter eggs baked in the dough.

Traditionally, Italians go to church on Good Friday at noon and mourn for three hours. Some people stay on their knees the whole time. The statues of the saints are covered with hoods. If you go into the old Italian neighborhoods you'll still see those traditions being observed.

Good Friday is a day of fasting. Then on Holy Saturday, everybody starts preparing for the big Easter feast. Easter dinner is always a seven- or eight-course meal, and we always eat baby lamb for the main course. We enjoy some of the same dishes for Easter that we do for Christmas, for example *struffoli,* which are little pieces of fried dough with honey drizzled on top and maybe some fresh raspberries or candied almonds. There's *pizza rustica,* which is actually an Italian version of a quiche with different meats like salami or prosciutto inside, and *pizza di grano,* which is the sweet winter wheat pie.

The Saints

In summer and early fall come the different saints' holidays. San Gennaro, the patron saint of Naples, is honored with a big festival in Manhattan's Little Italy in September. Then there's the festival for Santa Rosalia on 18th Avenue in Brooklyn. She's a Sicilian saint, who has a beautiful church in Bensonhurst that was built by the blood, sweat, and tears of the immigrants.

Another late-summer festival honors Our Lady of Mt. Carmel in Williamsburg, Brooklyn. It's the last place in America where they still practice the dance of the *giglio*—a five-story tower that carries a live band and a statue of the saint on top. It takes 121 men to carry the *giglio* and it's a big honor to be picked for the job. The men wear red caps and colorful costumes and dance the *giglio* all over the neighborhood for four hours. At the beginning, the monsignor blesses the tower and then a *capo*, an older man or leader from the neighborhood who probably carried the *giglio* for at least 20 years, comes out with a cane and gestures for the music to start.

The crowd gets excited; people run up and pin money on the *giglio*. The *capo* yells out the

commands in Italian. He'll stop the music suddenly, then he'll start it again. Then

he'll yell out another command and the 121 guys will drop the *giglio* and pick it right back up

again. It weighs four tons. Everybody cheers

and they pin more money onto the *giglio*.

The street festivals stem from the

worship of our patron saints, but as always food

is a huge factor. After all, what's a festival but

a big celebration in the street, and what's a

celebration without food? There are stands

everywhere that sell sausage

and peppers, fried dough, and all kinds of

specialties, such St. Anthony's Day Fried Cheese.

Baccala with Potatoes and Olives

I had an Aunt Mary who used to host Christmas Eve dinner at her house. She cooked *baccala*, or salt cod, four or five different ways—in tomato sauce, as a salad, in croquettes. I think this was one of the best preparations.

Note that the *baccala* needs to be soaked for an entire day in advance and the water changed several times.

Serves 4 as a main dish

1 pound dried salt cod, cut into 4 x 4-inch pieces

½ cup olive oil

3 onions, sliced

3 pounds Idaho potatoes, peeled and cut into ¼-inch dice

4 cups chicken or fish stock

1 tablespoon fresh thyme

2 tablespoons chopped fresh Italian parsley

1 cup Sicilian green olives, pitted and sliced

salt and pepper to taste

Soak the cod in cold water for 24 hours. Change the water 5 times to remove the salt. Drain and pat the cod pieces dry with a towel.

Heat the olive oil in a large pan over medium-high heat. Add the cod to the pan (do not overcrowd) and brown on one side. Carefully flip with a spatula and brown the other side. Once browned, remove the cod from the pan. Drain on paper towels and set aside in a warm spot.

Brown the onions in the same pan that the cod was cooked in. Once the onions are nicely browned, add the potatoes and cook until the potatoes are also browned. (If the pan is too dry, add a few drops of chicken stock.)

Once the potatoes have browned, add the rest of the chicken stock and bring the liquid to a boil. Lower the heat and allow to simmer for 5 minutes, then mix in the thyme, parsley, and olives.

Lay the browned cod on top of the potato mixture, cover, and cook for 10 minutes. Turn the cod over carefully and cook for 10 minutes more. Remove carefully to a warm platter using a spatula and serve immediately.

Caciucco Natale

CHRISTMAS FISH STEW

Caciucco is a fish stew similar to the *brodetto* in Chapter 3, but this one has quite a bit less liquid. You can use just one or two types of fish for this recipe, or you can use many more, depending upon what's fresh and available.

½ cup extra virgin olive oil

1 clove garlic, chopped

¼ teaspoon crushed red pepper flakes

½ pound squid, cleaned (see page 88) and cut
  into ½-inch dice

½ cup dry white wine

3 tablespoons tomato paste

4 cups water

1 teaspoon salt

1 pound cod fillet, skinless and boneless, cut into
  ½-inch dice

½ pound halibut, skinless and boneless, cut into
  ½-inch dice

½ pound shrimp, peeled, deveined, and cut into
  ½-inch pieces

½ pound sea scallops, halved

4 slices Italian bread, toasted and rubbed with a
  clove of garlic

Heat the olive oil in a soup pot over medium heat.
Add the garlic and pepper flakes and sauté. Add
the squid and cook for 30 minutes until tender.
Add the wine and continue to cook until it evaporates. Add the tomato paste, water, and salt.
Bring to a boil, add the cod and halibut and cook
for 15 minutes, adding more water if necessary.
Finish by adding the shrimp and the scallops and
cook for 5 minutes. Place 1 slice of garlic bread
in each soup dish and ladle a portion of the
caciucco over it. Serve immediately.

Christmas Eve Eel

We ate eel once a year, always on Christmas Eve.
You may have to go to an Italian or Greek fish
store to find eel; have the fish monger kill and skin
them for you, since they are very slippery.

Serve this dish with boiled potatoes or rice.

Serves 4 as a first course or main dish

¾ cup olive oil

2½ pounds eel, large variety, cut into 4-inch-
  long pieces

¾ cup flour

1 onion, thinly sliced

8 anchovy fillets, rinsed and chopped

3 cloves garlic, thinly sliced

½ pound white mushrooms, washed and sliced

1 teaspoon salt

1 teaspoon ground white pepper

1 cup dry white wine

1 tablespoon tomato sauce

3 cups frozen peas, thawed

½ cup chicken stock (see Basic Recipes, page 216)

Heat the olive oil in a sauté pan over medium-
high heat.

Roll the eel in the flour and fry until well
browned all around. Remove from the pan and
keep hot. Add the onion to the same pan and
sauté until light brown. Add the anchovies, garlic, mushrooms, salt, and pepper and cook for

5 minutes. Add the wine and cook until the wine has evaporated. Put the eel back in the pan, add the tomato sauce, peas, and chicken stock. Cover and cook for 30 minutes, adding more stock if needed. Remove the eel to a warm platter and spoon the sauce on top. The meat is very tender and will flake right off the bone.

Pizza di Grano

GRAIN PIE

This is one of my favorite desserts in the world. It's traditional for Christmas and Easter and one of the main reasons I look forward to the holidays. It's a time-consuming recipe, but well worth the effort.

Serves 8 to 10 for dessert

Pastry cream

2 tablespoons cornstarch

2 cups milk

½ cup sugar

2 eggs

1 egg yolk

1 vanilla bean, split lengthwise

2 tablespoons butter

Crust

3 cups flour

½ cup sugar

¼ teaspoon salt

½ teaspoon baking powder

¼ pound cold butter, cut into ¼-inch dice

2 eggs

1 egg yolk

Filling

candied peel of 1 orange and 1 lemon (see Basic Recipes, page 216), diced

½ cup hulled wheat berries or cooked bulgar wheat

1 cup ricotta cheese

½ cup sugar

2 eggs

1 egg yolk

3 drops orange flower water

To make the pastry cream: Dissolve the cornstarch in ¼ cup of the milk and set aside. Place the remaining 1¾ cups milk in a stainless steel saucepan with the vanilla bean and the sugar. Bring the mixture to a boil. In a bowl, combine the eggs and the cornstarch mixture. Gradually pour the boiled milk into the egg mixture while whisking well. Place it back on the stove over low heat. Continue to whisk until the mixture again comes to a boil and has thickened. Remove from the heat and add the butter. Whisk well. Remove the vanilla bean. Place the mixture in a bowl, cover the surface of the pastry cream with plastic wrap, and refrigerate.

To make the crust: In a large bowl, sift together all of the dry ingredients. Add the cold butter and rub the mixture between the palms of your hands until the butter pieces are incorporated and the flour mixture turns grainy. Form a well in the flour mixture with your fingers. Using a pastry cutter and your hands, mix and knead the dough until it forms a coarse ball. If the mixture is too dry, add a few drops of water; if too wet, add flour. Lightly butter and flour a 9-inch cake pan and reserve. Flour your working surface. Roll out the dough until it is 1/8-inch thick. Cut it into a circle that is 3 inches wider than the cake pan. Place the crust carefully in the cake pan, leaving a 1/2-inch overhang. Refrigerate. Take the remaining scraps of dough and form into a flat rectangle. Place between two sheets of plastic wrap and roll until 1/8-inch thick. Slice the dough with the tip of a small knife into 1/2-inch-wide strips and refrigerate.

Preheat the oven to 350° F.

To make the filling: Combine all the filling ingredients along with the pastry cream in a large bowl. Pour the filling into the prepared crust mold. Remove the plastic from the strips of dough and arrange across the tart to form a lattice pattern. Trim the edges of the strips and cover them by pinching with one or two long pieces along the edge of the tart. Chill for 10 to 15 minutes. Bake for 40 to 45 minutes, until a toothpick inserted in the pie removes cleanly. Cool completely and refrigerate before serving.

Panegocci

CHESTNUT PANCAKES

These chestnut pancakes are a staple in my family as a holiday antipasto. They are very versatile and can be served with salami, prosciutto, cheese, or pickled vegetables. In the fall, when we hunt or go mushroom-picking, we always bring these along as a snack. The condiment recipe I offer here is quick and easy. If you choose to use it, make sure to have all the ingredients ready and make it just before serving. (By the way, don't forget another serving option for the pancakes—at breakfast with syrup.)

Serves 4 as a snack, appetizer, or for breakfast

Pancakes

1 1/2 cups all-purpose flour

1 cup chestnut flour

2 teaspoons baking powder

1 teaspoon baking soda

1 teaspoon salt

1 egg, lightly beaten

2 1/4 cups milk

3 tablespoons vegetable oil

1 tablespoon butter

Condiment

1/2 cup extra virgin olive oil

1 cup grated aged pecorino cheese

1/4 cup ricotta cheese

freshly ground black pepper

To make the pancakes: Mix all the dry ingredients together and sift into a large bowl. Mix the egg, milk, and oil together and add to the flour mixture. Don't overmix. In a heavy skillet that is lightly greased with the butter over medium-high heat, drop enough batter in the center to make a pancake 6 inches across. Cook for 1 minute, flip and cook for 1 minute on the other side. Repeat to make more pancakes. Transfer to warm plates and serve. If you decide to use the condiment, mix all the ingredients together quickly and spoon onto the pancakes just before serving.

Holiday Spiced Nuts

These nuts are a Christmas tradition in my family. As kids, we would always try to eat them fresh out of the oven and would end up burning the roofs of our mouths.

Serves 5 to 10 as a snack or appetizer with aperitif

3 tablespoons unsalted butter

1½ tablespoons chopped orange zest

1½ tablespoons chopped lemon zest

1 teaspoon ground cinnamon

1½ teaspoons ground coriander

1 teaspoon ground mace

pinch of cayenne

2 tablespoons brown sugar

¾ teaspoon salt

2½ cups pecan halves

1½ cups whole blanched almonds

Preheat the oven to 300° F. In a large skillet, melt the butter over medium heat. Add the orange and lemon zest, cinnamon, coriander, mace, cayenne, brown sugar, and salt. Cook the mixture until bubbly and well blended. Add the nuts and stir to coat evenly. Transfer to a baking sheet and spread them out evenly. Bake for 35 minutes, stirring every 7 minutes until golden brown. Remove the nuts to a bowl and allow to cool. Leave them out and see how long they last.

Roasted Pork Loin with Fennel and Potatoes

I am an advocate of cooking meats on the bone, because they retain more flavor and stay moist and tender (plus you can use the bones later to make a broth or base for a soup). The garlic-rosemary paste perfumes this whole dish—and your kitchen—as it cooks.

I find that a lot of people have never tried fennel because they're not sure what to do with it. Fennel is great braised, as in this recipe; but before you cook it try a slice of it raw if you've never tasted it. It's terrific. You can add it raw to a green salad or just eat it alone with a little bit of extra virgin olive oil, red wine vinegar, salt, and pepper. Many Italians eat wedges of raw fennel after meals because they believe it aids digestion.

Serves 4 as a main course

Pork

4 cloves garlic

1 tablespoon finely chopped fresh rosemary

3 tablespoons fennel seed

salt and pepper to taste

2-pound piece of pork loin, bones split (ask your butcher to do this)

3 onions, quartered

¼ cup extra virgin olive oil

½ cup chicken stock (see Basic Recipes, page 216)

12 fresh bay leaves

12 small red potatoes, halved

½ cup dry white wine

Fennel

3 large fennel bulbs, tops removed and discarded, cut in vertical slices ½-inch thick

⅓ cup extra virgin olive oil

2 cups chicken stock

¼ cup dry white wine

juice of ½ lemon

salt and pepper to taste

To make the pork: Preheat the oven to 350° F.

Chop the garlic and rosemary together with a knife until they form a paste. Add the fennel seed, salt, and pepper, mixing well. Stuff the mixture into the cut in the pork where the bones were split. Place the pork and the onions in a roasting pan. Drizzle the olive oil over the pork and pour the chicken stock into the bottom of the pan. Roast for ½ hour.

Place a bay leaf between each potato half and season with salt and pepper. After the pork has cooked for ½ hour, place the potatoes in the same pan as the pork. Continue to cook for 1 hour.

To make the fennel: While the pork is roasting, place the fennel in a covered saucepan with the olive oil, chicken stock, wine, lemon juice, salt, and pepper. Simmer over low heat for 40 minutes or until the fennel is tender.

When the pork is done, remove the pan from the oven. (To test the pork for doneness, stick a fork or skewer in the thickest part of the meat then press down; if the juice runs clear it's done. I like my pork tender and still a little pink, but most people prefer it more well-done.) Spoon off the excess fat, remove the pork to a warm platter, and allow to rest for about 8 minutes. Place the pan drippings and the onions in a saucepan with the ½ cup of wine, cook for 3 minutes, then keep warm. Cut the pork into thin slices and serve with the potatoes and fennel on the side, spooning some sauce around each plate. You can leave the bay leaves in the potatoes—it's a festive touch—but be sure not to eat them. They're tough and dry.

Abbacchio al Forno

ROASTED SUCKLING LAMB

This dish always was—and still is—the center-piece of Easter Sunday dinner. My family would buy the lamb live in a market near DeKalb Avenue in Brooklyn. The meat is fork-tender and delicious, and in my family not one bit of it goes to waste. The head was always my grandfather's favorite and he would take great pleasure in grossing out all the children by making a show of eating it in front of us. If you find the head too distasteful, you can let your butcher keep it; the dish is just as good without it.

Serves 10 as a main course

1 12 to 14 pound whole lamb (ask your butcher to cut the lamb into quarters, crack all the joints and split the head in half)

⅓ cup extra virgin olive oil

3 heads garlic, separated into cloves

¾ cup fresh rosemary

salt and freshly ground black pepper

3½ pounds small new potatoes, quartered

½ pound fresh white *cipolline* onions

2 cups dry white wine

Preheat the oven to 375° F. Rinse the lamb with cold water and pat dry. Trim off the excess fat, leaving a thin layer to protect the meat during cooking. Rub the lamb with 3 tablespoons of the olive oil.

Using a small knife, make small incisions all over the lamb. Cut half the garlic cloves into thin slices. Slip the slices into the incisions with half the rosemary. Season the lamb with salt and pepper. Sprinkle a little garlic, rosemary, salt, and pepper on the head. Cover the brain with aluminum foil.

Place the lamb bone-side down in a large roasting pan, leaving room for the potatoes, onions, and head. Crush the remaining garlic, scatter over the lamb and roast for 40 minutes.

Place the head cut side up in the pan. Add the potatoes and onions and toss with the pan drippings. Pour the wine over the lamb and continue to roast. Baste periodically with the pan juices and cook for another 45 minutes, until fork-tender.

Remove the lamb from the oven to a serving platter, cover, and allow to rest for 15 to 20 minutes. Leave the potatoes and onions in the pan and return to the oven for an additional 15 minutes or until tender.

To serve, cut the lamb at the joints, add the head to the platter, spoon the pan juices over the meat, and serve with the potatoes and onions on the side.

Black Olive and Rosemary Focaccia

This focaccia is wonderful served during a meal or as an *antipasto*, dipped in some extra virgin olive oil. It's also great for sandwiches and freezes very well. The next time you have hamburgers, try this instead of the traditional hamburger bun.

Serves 6 to 12 as an appetizer or side dish

Sponge

2 cups plus 1 tablespoon flour

2 envelopes active dry yeast

1¼ cups hot water

pinch of salt

Dough

1¾ cups flour

21 large Calabrese olives, pitted and coarsely chopped

2 tablespoons fresh rosemary, chopped

4 tablespoons unsalted butter, at room temperature

salt and pepper to taste

8 tablespoons olive oil

coarse salt

To make the sponge: Place 2 cups of the flour in a medium-size bowl and make a well in the center. In a smaller bowl, dissolve the yeast in the water, stirring with a wooden spoon. Then pour the dissolved yeast into the well of the flour, add the salt and stir until all the flour is incorporated. Sprinkle the remaining tablespoon of flour over the sponge. Cover the bowl with a dish towel and let the sponge rest in a warm place until it has doubled in size, about 1 hour.

To make the dough: When the sponge is ready, spread the flour all over a board then spread the sponge over it, along with two-thirds of the chopped olives, the rosemary, butter, salt, and pepper. Start mixing the dough with your hands, incorporating all the flour, and knead until all the butter is completely dissolved.

Use 4 tablespoons of the oil to generously grease a 12 x 13-inch nonstick lasagna pan. Using a rolling pin or your hands, stretch the dough into a rectangle that is the same size as the pan. Transfer the dough to the prepared pan, drizzle the remaining 4 tablespoons oil on top. Prick the dough with a fork. Cover with a towel and let rest in a warm place until it doubles in size, about 30 minutes.

Preheat the oven to 375° F. When the dough is ready, press the remaining olive pieces into the dough and sprinkle on some coarse salt. Bake for 40 minutes, until golden brown, then remove from oven and allow to cool. Cut into 12 4-inch squares and serve.

Grissini with Olives and Oregano

These *grissini* or thin breadsticks are every Italian kid's favorite snack. They used to be the preamble to all our holiday meals. We would stuff ourselves on these, dipping them in olive oil while waiting for the food to come out. For adults, they are a perfect snack with cocktails or as an accompaniment to the meal. They can be made ahead and stored for up to a week.

Makes about 24

¾ **teaspoon fresh yeast**

1½ **cups lukewarm water**

1 **tablespoon olive oil**

1 **tablespoon sugar**

1¼ **cups bread flour**

6 **ounces Gaeta olives, finely chopped**

¼ **cup dried oregano**

1 **teaspoon salt**

1 **egg white**

Preheat the oven to 350° F.

Dissolve the yeast in the water, then add the remaining ingredients except for the salt and egg white and mix for about 4 minutes using a mixer with a dough hook on low speed or by hand. Add the salt and mix an additional 12 minutes. Put the dough in a lightly oiled bowl, cover with a damp towel, and place in a warm spot (75 to 80° F.) until it doubles in size. Punch down the dough and cut into approximately 24 pieces, about 2 tablespoons each. Roll each piece with both hands on a flour-free surface until 12 inches long. Brush with egg white, place on a sheet pan to rest for 30 minutes, then bake for 45 minutes, until golden brown. Remove the *grissini* from the oven and place on a platter, allowing them to dry before serving.

Three Types of Flour

There are three basic types of flour: high-gluten flour, which can be made into a very pliable, stretchy dough, for kneading and shaping breads; all-purpose flour, which is medium-gluten; and low-gluten or cake flour, which is smoother and comes out lighter and fluffier for cakes.

Pizza Rustica

MEAT PIE

You may be surprised to find that this is not the "pizza pie" you are accustomed to. It is more like a quiche. It can be served warm or cold and makes a great midnight snack.

Serves 6 as an appetizer, lunch, or snack

Dough

3 cups flour

2 teaspoons baking powder

$\frac{1}{2}$ cup cold butter, cut into small cubes

$\frac{1}{2}$ teaspoon salt

4 to 5 tablespoons ice water

3 eggs, slightly beaten

Filling

4 cups ricotta cheese

$1\frac{1}{2}$ pounds mozzarella cheese, shredded

$\frac{1}{4}$ cup grated pecorino cheese

7 eggs, slightly beaten

$\frac{1}{2}$ pound Sicilian salami with peppercorns, diced

$\frac{1}{2}$ pound pepperoni, diced

2 ounces prosciutto, diced

1 bunch or $\frac{1}{2}$ cup fresh Italian parsley, chopped

To make the dough: Sift the flour and the baking powder together. Quickly mix the sifted ingredients with the butter and cut with a pizza cutter until the butter is in tiny pieces. Mound the mixture together and make a well in the center. Place the salt, 4 tablespoons of the water, and the eggs in the well. Gradually start to combine all the ingredients with your hands. Add more water if the mixture is too dry and does not come together. Knead and form it into a ball. Dust your work surface with flour. With a rolling pin, roll the dough into a circle until it is about 3 inches wider than a 9-inch springform pan. Pick up the dough by rolling it around the rolling pin, then unroll it right into the pan. This way you avoid handling it and possibly puncturing it. Line the pan with the dough and refrigerate until needed.

Preheat the oven to 350° F.

To make filling: Mix the 3 cheeses and the eggs together in a large bowl. Add the diced salami, pepperoni, and prosciutto and mix. Mix in the parsley. Spread the mixture into the dough-lined baking pan and bake for 45 minutes, until a toothpick inserted in the pie removes cleanly. Remove from the oven, allow to cool to room temperature, cut into wedges, and serve.

St. Anthony's Day Fried Cheese

It seems that every saint has a feast day in an Italian-American neighborhood somewhere. This dish is a tradition in our house on St. Anthony's Day, in early June. This recipe calls for *caciocavallo*, a firm cow's milk cheese that is very popular in Southern Italy. You may substitute mozzarella if you wish. Fried Cheese is wonderful with a crusty piece of bread, as a hot antipasto, or as a snack in the afternoon.

Serves 6 as an appetizer or snack

⅓ **cup virgin olive oil**

4 cloves garlic, crushed

1½ **pounds caciocavallo, rind removed, cut into**
   ½-**inch slices**

¼ **cup red wine vinegar**

1 teaspoon fresh oregano

salt and freshly ground black pepper to taste

Heat the olive oil in a sauté pan large enough to fit all the cheese over high heat. Add the garlic and sauté until golden brown. Remove the garlic and add the slices of cheese. Sauté until golden brown, then turn and sauté on other side until golden brown. Don't allow to melt. Add the vinegar, oregano, salt, and pepper. Cook for 1 minute more, remove from the pan, drain on paper towels, and serve immediately on small plates or dishes.

Struffoli

FRIED DOUGH BITS WITH HONEY, HAZELNUTS, AND RASPBERRIES

This is a very sweet dessert, which, as far as I know, is Neapolitan in origin. This dish is a special treat for kids of all ages during the Christmas holiday season, but beware: They will eat this dish with their fingers, which will become *very sticky!*

Serves 6 as a dessert or snack

Dough

3½ cups flour

2 teaspoons baking powder

3 tablespoons sugar

1½ teaspoons vanilla extract

4 eggs

2 egg yolks

¼ cup vegetable oil

about 4 cups vegetable oil for frying

Topping

1 tablespoon butter, softened

1½ cups whole hazelnuts

1 teaspoon egg white, lightly beaten

½ cup granulated sugar

½ cup honey

1 pint raspberries

confectioners' sugar for dusting

To make the dough: Set up a mixer with a hook attachment. Place the flour, baking powder, and sugar in the bowl and mix it well. Add the vanilla, eggs, and ¼ cup oil and work it until it comes together like a dough. (Alternatively perform these steps with your hands.) Remove the mixture from the bowl and divide in half. Roll the pieces with your hands into cylinders and keep rolling until you have long tubes, ½ inch in diameter. Repeat with the other half of dough. Cut the tubes into ¾-inch pieces. Pour the 4 cups oil into a deep skillet. Heat oil to 375° F. Deep fry the *struffoli* until puffed and golden colored, about 2½ minutes. Drain on paper towels.

To make the topping: Preheat the oven to 325° F. Grease an 11 x 17-inch baking pan with the butter.

In a bowl, mix the hazelnuts with the egg white. Drain the excess egg white then roll the nuts in the granulated sugar to coat. Place the nuts in the baking pan and toast in the oven for about 30 minutes. When nicely toasted, allow to cool slightly. (Caution: the nuts are very hot.) Mound the fried dough pieces onto a serving platter. Sprinkle the hazelnuts over them, then coat the entire dish with the honey. Arrange the raspberries nicely around the edge of the platter, sprinkle with confectioners' sugar, and serve.

Potato Cake with Meat Ragu and Peas

Many people have elaborate specialties they like to serve on New Year's Eve, fancy dishes like caviar and oysters, which were alien to me when I was growing up. This simple, delicious, and hearty peasant dish was always served on New Year's Eve in my family. It's a little bit like a beef pot pie or a shepherd's pie, Italian style, but not quite because it doesn't have any pastry. The "riced" potato mixture takes the place of the pastry, which I guess is why we call it Potato Cake.

Serves 6 to 8 as a first course or main dish

¼ cup olive oil

1 onion, chopped

1 clove garlic, minced

1 pound ground beef

1 stalk celery, chopped

½ cup dry white wine

⅓ cup tomato paste, diluted with 1 cup water

½ cup peas

½ cup boiled ham, diced

1 cup caciocavallo cheese, diced (mozzarella is an acceptable substitute)

¼ cup chopped fresh Italian parsley

salt and pepper to taste

4½ pounds Idaho potatoes, peeled

7 tablespoons butter

2 eggs

4 cups grated Parmesan cheese

½ cup breadcrumbs

Heat the olive oil in a skillet over medium heat. Sauté the onion and garlic for 4 minutes, until translucent. Add the beef and sauté for about 8 minutes, until the meat is browned. Add the celery and wine and cook until the wine evaporates. Add the tomato paste, lower the heat, and cook for 20 minutes. The mixture should be dry, not watery.

Add the peas, ham, caciocavallo cheese, and parsley and remove from the heat. Season with salt and pepper.

Boil the potatoes in salted water until tender. Drain and "rice" them into a large bowl using an old-fashioned food mill *(passatutto)*. Add 6 tablespoons of the butter, the eggs, Parmesan cheese, and salt and pepper to taste. Combine well.

Preheat the oven to 425° F. Grease a 10-inch springform pan well with the remaining tablespoon butter. Sprinkle with half the breadcrumbs. Using three-quarters of the potato mixture, cover the bottom and sides of the pan. Spoon the beef mixture into the center. Cover with the remaining potato mixture. Sprinkle the top with the remaining breadcrumbs.

Bake for 20 minutes. Reduce the oven to 325° and continue to bake for another 20 minutes, until golden brown. Remove from the oven, let stand for 10 minutes, and serve.

Anna Amendolara Nurse

The Teacher

If you want kind, patient, caring advice on cooking—Italian-American or otherwise—go to Anna Amendolara Nurse.

Anna was born in Middle Village, Queens, on the outskirts of Brooklyn, but she's lived in Brooklyn for as long as she can remember. She learned to cook from her mother, Rosa Amendolara, who was from Grumo near Bari. "I started cooking at age four or five when I boiled my first egg," she says. "My mother was a fantastic cook and I was always in the kitchen watching her, my grandmothers, and my aunts cook."

Anna still does a Christmas dinner for 35. She does all the cooking herself, Christmas Eve and then again Christmas Day. It's a lot of work, but it's worth it, she says. Relatives come from all over the country to celebrate on Christmas Eve in the European style. The meal starts with antipasti around 6 P.M. and stretches until it's time to go to midnight Mass. Afterward everyone's welcome to come back for a late snack. It's a huge meal, a celebration, and an indulgence, with one basic rule: "Only fish and seafood."

The appetizers might include boiled or fried shrimp, fried calamari, a *baccala* salad, and baked clams. The sit-down portion of the meal begins with two pasta dishes: one with a red sauce, perhaps with lobster and/or crab claws; the other a classic white clam sauce, or maybe a mussels-and-white-wine sauce. "For those pasta dishes, do not use cappellini," she insists. "Cappellini are angel hair and they were not invented for pasta dishes. They were invented for soups. Use linguine or spaghetti or spaghettini but never cappellini."

The main course might include stuffed cuttlefish or stuffed lobster and/or steamed or boiled lobster. "Years ago, we used to always eat eel," she says, "but now a lot of people turn their nose up at it, which is really too bad." Anna recalls Christmas Eve eels cut up into 2-inch pieces, the skin still on, and broiled with some lemon or vinegar, a bay leaf, and some good olive oil. The leftovers were put in a crock with fresh garlic, fresh bay leaf, fresh pars-ley, and red wine vinegar then left for a week and, *presto*, you had pickled eels to serve as an *antipasto* on New Year's Eve.

The Christmas Eve side dish would be a green vegetable, usually broccoli rabe, which didn't used to be as popular as it is now. There would also be a green salad. The meal would finish up with traditional desserts, Italian cheesecake, cookies, fruits in season, apples, and oranges. Then it was time to go to Mass.

Anna started out as a dramatic soprano. She had her Carnegie Hall debut in 1953 and once sang at the Waldorf Astoria for Eleanor Roosevelt. She retired from the stage after she married Eugene Stanley Anthony Nurse and began to raise a family. Later she became a professional cooking teacher, starting at her church's adult education program. Anna has received many awards and honors for her teaching and is on the advisory board of the James Beard Foundation. She still works miracles regularly in her Brooklyn kitchen.

I don't know how many chefs, professional or otherwise, she's trained or inspired, but I do know there wouldn't be nearly as many good ones out there if it wasn't for Anna Nurse.

Anna and I prepare an afternoon snack of linguine with garlic and olive oil.

olci

Like many people, I love sweets. I have my own special favorite desserts: *pizza di grano, struf-*

foli, crisp biscotti for dipping in a cup of coffee. Lucky for me, Italian-American cooking is rich

with desserts, from the gorgeous marzipan, a Sicilian specialty that makes a

perfect gift for special occasions, to the rustic wheat pies—from the extremely simple to the

complicated and involved.

Of all the pastry in America, I think the Italian-American is among the best known

and the best tasting. Sicilian pastries are a marvel. Italians also make the richest, most irresistible

handmade ice cream in the world, and this tradition has been carried over by the immigrants.

No Italian family would ever come to a feast, gathering, celebration, casual dinner, or even just a cordial visit empty handed. Ninety-nine times out of one hundred, they would arrive with some kind of dessert or pastry as a gift, whether they baked it specifically for the occasion or made a quick stop at the pastry shop to pick it up along the way. Any time Italian-Americans have a decent-size gathering, we always end the meal with dozens of different kinds of pastry—*tortas* or cakes, cannoli, cookies, cheesecake, and so forth—on the table. On these occasions you always have to be prepared for a special dessert, even if a lot went before it.

Different regions have their specialties, but a few desserts, like *zabaglione* or *semifreddo*, are universal. This chapter offers a representative sampling. Because I love desserts so much, I could have included many more recipes, but these are my favorites.

In a medium-size mixing bowl or with an electric mixer, whisk 1/4 cup of the sugar, the eggs, rum, nutmeg, and lemon zest until smooth. Add the milk and cream mixture. Mix until thoroughly blended. Pour over the bread and sprinkle the remaining 2 tablespoons of sugar over the mixture.

Place a large pan in the oven with about 1 inch of water in it and set the baking dish inside. Bake for 40 minutes or until a toothpick inserted in the pudding comes out clean. Set aside and allow to cool for 20 to 30 minutes.

Angie's Italian Crescent Cookies

Aunt Angie, my grandmother's younger aunt and sidekick, is a great cook who has some fantastic baking recipes. These cookies are one of her specialties, and all the kids in the family clamor for them. Rumor has it that my cousin Joe once gained 11 pounds from spending a weekend with Aunt Angie and eating so many of these cookies.

Yields about 45 cookies

1 cup unsalted butter, slightly softened

1/3 cup granulated sugar

2 teaspoons vanilla extract

2 1/4 cups flour

1/2 teaspoon salt

2 cups chopped walnuts

grated zest of 1 lemon

confectioners' sugar for dusting

In a bowl, mix the butter and sugar with a whisk or wooden spoon until well incorporated. Add the vanilla and 1/4 cup of water.

In another bowl, mix the flour, salt, nuts, and zest, and add them to the butter-sugar mixture. Blend with your hands until it comes together nicely. Place it between two sheets of plastic wrap, roll it about 1/4-inch thick, and refrigerate for about 45 minutes.

Preheat the oven to 325° F. Cut the cookie dough into moon shapes with a cookie cutter. Place on a parchment-lined cookie sheet and bake for 30 minutes, until golden brown. Allow to cool, dust with confectioners' sugar, and serve.

Chestnut and Ricotta Semifreddo

If you think ice cream is a special treat, wait till you try this. *Semifreddo* is a much-enriched ice cream, really a frozen mousse. In our family, chestnuts have always been a delicacy. Fresh chestnuts are available in the fall, so traditionally this is a fall or winter dessert—but it's too good to rule out completely in the spring and summer.

You can buy canned chestnuts, either whole or pureed. If whole, simply puree them in the food processor. If you want to use fresh chestnuts, you'll have to peel them open, boil or roast them, and then puree them. For the purposes of this recipe, it doesn't make much difference whether you use fresh or canned chestnuts. You'll also need an ice cream maker.

Serves 8

1¼ cups milk

2¼ cups sugar

3 tablespoons butter

½ cup dark rum

1 pound ricotta cheese

1½ pounds chestnut puree

¼ cup chopped candied lemon peel (see Basic Recipes, page 216)

In a saucepan over medium heat, combine the milk and ¼ cup of the sugar and heat until the sugar is dissolved. Set aside.

In a large stainless steel saucepan over low heat, combine the butter, the remaining 2 cups of sugar, the rum, and 1 cup of water and heat until the sugar is dissolved. Remove from the heat and stir in the ricotta, chestnut puree, and candied lemon peel. Mix in the reserved milk-sugar mixture.

Process in an ice cream maker, scoop into bowls, and serve immediately.

Candied Fruit

These little confections are great alongside coffee, with or without an assortment of cookies. You can dip them in chocolate or eat them as is.

Although they are very similar, Candied Fruit should not be confused with Candied Fruit Peel, which is a Basic Recipe (see page 216). Both recipes use only the peels of the fruit, so you can eat the insides.

Makes about 1 cup

3 cups sugar

2 grapefruits

2 oranges

In a large saucepan over medium heat, dissolve 2 cups of the sugar in 2 cups of water.

Quarter the fruits with a small paring knife. Remove the whole peel with your fingers. Slice the peels into about $1/4$-inch julienne. Add the peels to the sugar water and cook for about 8 to 10 minutes, or until tender.

Pour the remaining 1 cup of sugar over a cookie sheet. Carefully remove the fruit peels from the sugar water with a slotted spoon and allow to cool slightly. Place the fruit peels on the cookie sheet and toss them until they have a thick coating of sugar. Store in a jar, well covered, at room temperature.

Chocolate and Coffee Cream Tart

This recipe comes from my mother's family, so it is probably Neapolitan in origin. Chocolate is generally reserved for a special occasion or holiday, and this tart is perfect for those times. It is a time-consuming recipe, but it yields a rich treat that is well worth the effort.

Serves 8

Dough

$1^1/2$ tablespoons flour

$1/3$ cup sugar

grated zest of $1/2$ lemon

$2^1/2$ tablespoons cold butter, cut into small pieces

$1/3$ cup vegetable oil

Filling

$1^1/2$ tablespoons unflavored gelatin

$3^1/2$ ounces semisweet chocolate

$1/4$ cup espresso or strong coffee

$3/4$ cup milk

$1/3$ cup light brown sugar

$1/4$ teaspoon salt

2 egg yolks

1 teaspoon vanilla extract

$1/2$ teaspoon ground cinnamon

1 cup heavy cream

$1/4$ teaspoon cream of tartar

$1/4$ cup granulated sugar

$1/4$ cup apricot jam

chocolate shavings for garnish

To make the dough: In a mixing bowl, combine the flour, sugar, and lemon zest. Blend in the butter. Make a well in the center and add the oil, then mix until the dough just comes together. Wrap in plastic wrap and refrigerate for at least 30 minutes.

To make the filling: Combine the gelatin and $1/4$ cup cold water in a cup. Allow to sit for 10 minutes. Place the chocolate, espresso, and milk into a microwave-safe container. Microwave for 15 seconds at a time on high, stirring in between, until the mixture is completely liquid. Stir in the brown sugar, salt, egg yolks, vanilla, and cinnamon. Microwave again until the mixture is creamy and heavily coats the back of a spoon. Stir in the gelatin, allow to cool to room temperature, then chill in the fridge. (*Note*: if you don't have a microwave use a double boiler.)

Preheat the oven to 350° F.

Place the dough on a floured work surface and roll it out to fit a 9-inch tart pan. Line the pan with the dough, pressing it in carefully. Stick the dough with a fork, making 5 to 6 small holes right through it. Place parchment paper on top of the dough, then fill the pan with dried beans or rice and bake for 10 minutes. Remove the paper and beans or rice and bake the dough for 6 minutes more, or until golden brown. Remove and allow to cool.

In a mixing bowl, whisk together the heavy cream, cream of tartar, and granulated sugar until you have stiff peaks. Using a spatula, gently fold the cream into the chilled chocolate mixture.

To assemble: When the tart shell is cooled, spread a thin layer of the apricot jam on the bottom of the shell, then fill it with the chocolate cream. Cover loosely with plastic wrap and refrigerate for at least 2 to 3 hours. Garnish with chocolate shavings and serve.

Crispelle

FRIED DOUGH TREATS

When I was a kid, I went to Saint Jerome's Grammar School in the Flatbush section of Brooklyn. Junior Radarazzo was a good friend from my class and we used to "fish" on the subway gratings after school. We would take lead fishing sinkers, put a piece of chewing gum on the bottom, then lower them on a string through the gratings to pick up the change that people had dropped. After these fishing expeditions, we would go to Junior's house and his mother would feed us these simple fried dough treats topped with powdered sugar. They're called *crispelle* and are traditionally served at Christmastime, but you don't have to wait until then.

For an added festive touch, you can sprinkle the *crispelle* with candied confetti—little toasted colored sugar granules available in the bakery supply section of your supermarket. Use red and green for Christmas; red, white, and blue for the Fourth of July; and black, white, and orange for Halloween.

Makes about 2 dozen

$1^1/_2$ **cups flour, sifted**

1 teaspoon baking powder

2 large eggs

2 egg yolks

4 cups vegetable oil

$^1/_2$ **cup honey**

confectioners' sugar for garnish

In a large bowl, place the flour and baking powder and make a well in the center. Mix the eggs and yolks together and place in the well of the flour. Knead well for about 3 minutes. Allow to rest for 15 minutes.

On a floured work surface, roll the dough out to $\frac{1}{8}$-inch thickness. (Sprinkle the dough with a little extra flour to prevent it from sticking when you roll it.) Cut the dough into 1 x 3-inch strips using a pastry wheel, then fold them into bows.

In a saucepan, heat the oil over medium heat. Drop the bows into the oil and fry until golden brown. In a separate saucepan, heat the honey, then drizzle it over the *crispelle*. As an alternative, you can sprinkle them with confectioners' sugar.

Fried Ricotta

This is a dessert that appears only on the most important holidays—Christmas, Easter, a major birthday or anniversary celebration. It is an unusual way to use ricotta, a simple recipe that must be served and consumed immediately. This version calls for raisins, but you can have a little fun and substitute chocolate chips or candied fruit or whatever other confection you fancy.

Serves 6

½ pound macaroons, finely ground

2 cups ricotta cheese, drained of excess liquid in a strainer

¼ teaspoon ground cinnamon

2 tablespoons white raisins

3 eggs

1 cup breadcrumbs

1 cup vegetable oil

In a mixing bowl, combine the macaroons, ricotta, cinnamon, raisins, and 2 of the eggs. Mix until well-incorporated. Take 1 tablespoon of the mixture at a time and form into small balls. Beat the remaining egg well. Roll each ricotta ball in the egg and then in the breadcrumbs. Heat the vegetable oil in a small saucepan over medium-high heat. Fry the ricotta balls until golden brown, drain on paper towels, and serve immediately.

Cucidati

SICILIAN FIG COOKIES

I have a hunch this is where the idea for Fig Newtons originated, except that these are about a million times better. My aunt used to make these for holidays or special occasions, gift wrap them, and give them away.

Pastry

1¼ cups flour

1 teaspoon baking powder

¼ cup sugar

¼ cup cold unsalted butter, cut into small pieces

1 egg

1 tablespoon grated orange zest

Filling

½ cup dried figs, stemmed and coarsely chopped

½ cup dried currants (or dried cranberries)

¼ cup lightly chopped dark raisins

½ cup coarsely chopped walnuts

1 tablespoon brown sugar

1 teaspoon cocoa powder

¼ teaspoon ground mace

⅛ teaspoon ground cloves

⅛ teaspoon ground cinnamon

2 tablespoons grated orange zest

¼ cup honey

Preheat the oven to 375° F.

To make the pastry: In a large bowl, sift together the flour and the baking powder then combine with the sugar. Add the butter and cut in until the butter is incorporated with the flour. Once combined, make a well and place the egg and zest in the well. Using your fingers, gradually mix the egg and flour together. Knead until you have a smooth dough. Divide the dough into thirds and roll each piece into a rectangle ¼-inch thick. Wrap in plastic wrap or wax paper and refrigerate.

To make the filling: In a large bowl, combine all of the filling ingredients. Mix together with a spoon or an electric mixer on low speed until they are well blended. Divide the mixture into thirds. Take the prepared pastry doughs out of the fridge, remove the plastic or wax paper, and spoon an equal portion of the filling onto each one. Roll as you would a jelly roll. Bake for 15 minutes on a greased cookie sheet until golden brown. Allow to cool, then cut the baked rolls into 2-inch-wide cookies and serve.

Peach with Amaretti

Amaretto cookies—*amaretti* in the plural—are extremely popular in this country and are available in most supermarkets (see also the recipe on page 173). You can prepare the filling two or three days in advance, spoon it onto the peach halves, then keep them in the fridge until you're ready to bake.

Serves 2

5 amaretto cookies, crushed

2 tablespoons white rum

1 egg yolk

1 teaspoon sugar

1 ripe peach, halved and pitted

Preheat the oven to 375° F.

Mix the cookies, rum, egg yolk, and sugar together until they form a paste. Spoon the mixture over the peach halves. Place in a baking dish. Bake for 30 minutes, and serve.

Peaches in Red Wine, Tuscan Style

This dish should always be served at room temperature, so allow plenty of time for it to cool. It goes particularly well with Crescent Cookies (see page 175).

Serves 4

2 pounds ripe peaches

2 cups good red wine, preferably from Tuscany

$\frac{1}{2}$ cup sugar

1 vanilla bean, split

$\frac{1}{4}$ cup whole roasted almonds, shelled

1 tablespoon julienned fresh mint

Plunge the peaches into a generous amount of boiling water for 1 minute. Remove and refresh in ice water for about 1 minute. Carefully remove the skins by hand. Slice the peaches in half and remove the pits.

In a saucepan, heat the wine, sugar, and vanilla bean. Bring to a boil and simmer for 3 minutes.

Place the peaches and almonds in a bowl. Pour the hot wine over the top. Allow to stand and return to room temperature, about 30 minutes. Sprinkle with the mint and serve.

Pan Forte di Siena

SIENA FRUITCAKE

This delicacy is a cross between candy and fruit-cake. It originated in the beautiful Tuscan hill town of Siena and is very popular as a gift around the winter holidays. When prepared correctly, it is outrageously delicious and can become habit forming.

Serves 8

1 cup coarsely chopped walnuts

1 cup whole almonds

³/₄ cup chopped candied orange peel (see Basic Recipes, page 216)

³/₄ cup chopped candied lemon peel (see Basic Recipes, page 216)

1 teaspoon ground cinnamon

¹/₂ teaspoon anise seed

¹/₄ teaspoon ground cloves

¹/₄ teaspoon nutmeg

¹/₂ cup flour

¹/₂ cup honey

¹/₂ cup brown sugar

3 tablespoons unsalted butter

Preheat the oven to 300° F.

In a large bowl, combine the walnuts, almonds, candied peels, cinnamon, anise seed, ground cloves, nutmeg, and flour. Reserve. In a small saucepan, heat the honey, brown sugar, and butter. Bring to a boil, then continue to cook for 4 to 5 minutes over medium-low heat. Carefully combine with the reserved nut mixture.

Pour the mixture onto an oiled cookie sheet. Flatten to ¹/₄ inch with a metal spatula and bake for 45 minutes. Allow to cool, cut into 2-inch squares, and serve. The *pan forte* can be stored, covered, at room temperature, for up to 2 weeks.

Peach and Bread Cake

God forbid my grandmother should ever throw anything away. I think she has more recipes for leftovers than anything else. This one makes use of leftover bread, and since we can't have a meal without fresh bread, there is always plenty left over. This cake is good with fruit salad, ice cream, or sorbet on the side, or just by itself.

Serves 6

6 ounces stale bread, cut into ¹/₂-inch cubes

1 cup milk

2 eggs

1 cup granulated sugar

2¹/₄ pounds ripe peaches, halved, peeled, and sliced

30 seedless grapes, halved

2 tablespoons dark rum

finely grated zest of 1 lemon

1 tablespoon melted unsalted butter

¼ cup white breadcrumbs

confectioners' sugar for dusting

Preheat the oven to 350° F.

In a bowl, soften the bread in the milk and squeeze it dry. Beat the eggs and ¾ cup of the granulated sugar in a mixing bowl until frothy. Add the bread and mix well. Add the peaches, grapes, rum, and lemon zest.

Generously butter a 12 x 14-inch rectangular mold and dust with half the breadcrumbs. Pour in cake mixture, sprinkle with the remaining ¼ cup granulated sugar, the remaining breadcrumbs, and the melted butter. Bake for 30 minutes, until a toothpick inserted in the center of the cake removes cleanly. Allow to cool. Cut into squares, garnish by dusting liberally with confectioners' sugar, and serve.

Batter-Fried Cantaloupe

Rather than serving cantaloupe in wedges or cut up in fruit salad, why not try frying the fruit? It's important to use a ripe, unbruised melon—soft to the touch and very fragrant at the stem. This dessert should be eaten immediately.

Serves 4

1 small cantaloupe

2 tablespoons granulated sugar

½ cup crème de menthe liqueur (white or green)

2 tablespoons flour

½ cup white wine

1 teaspoon olive oil

pinch of salt

1 egg white, beaten until stiff peaks form

1 cup vegetable oil

1½ tablespoons confectioners' sugar

Cut the melon in half, remove the seeds, and cut it into ¼-inch wedges. Remove the skin and place the wedges in a bowl. Sprinkle with the granulated sugar and liqueur. Allow to stand for 1 hour.

In another bowl, mix the flour, wine, oil, and salt. Gently fold in the egg white. Remove the melon wedges from the liqueur and dip them in the egg white mixture. Heat the vegetable oil in a skillet over medium-high heat. Fry the melon wedges until lightly golden in color. Remove and drain on paper towels. Dust with the confectioners' sugar and serve immediately.

Sicilian Citrus Granita

This recipe for Italian ice is completely idiot-proof. It's also very refreshing. If you go to the Little Italy street festivals in late summer, you'll see vendors with carts shaving blocks of frozen *granita* into cups. Often it's just shaved ice with a syrup poured into it, though, so look for the real thing.

Serves 6

2 cups water

3/4 cup sugar

1/2 cup lemon juice

1/2 cup orange juice

1 tablespoon grenadine

In a bowl, mix all the ingredients together and place the mixture in a metal pan. Put it in the freezer until well frozen. Once frozen, shave with a spoon and serve with seasonal mixed berries.

Sesame Seed Cookies

If you go into any self-respecting Italian pastry shop, you'll find mountains of these cookies—delicious little nuggets that are a wonderful tradition on holidays, birthdays, and especially at weddings. And they make a perfect gift.

Makes 3 dozen

3 cups flour

3/4 cup sugar

2 teaspoons baking powder

1/8 teaspoon salt

8 tablespoons unsalted butter, softened

2 eggs, lightly beaten

1/4 cup milk

2 1/2 teaspoons vanilla extract

1 cup sesame seeds

Preheat the oven to 375° F.

Sift the flour, sugar, baking powder, and salt into a large mixing bowl. Mix in the butter until the mixture resembles a coarse meal. Don't overmix. Make a well in the center and add the eggs, milk, and vanilla. Mix until everything is incorporated and you have a smooth dough. Again, don't overmix.

Divide the dough into 4 pieces. Roll each piece into a long log 1/2-inch in diameter. Cut the logs into 2-inch pieces. Brush each piece with water and roll in the sesame seeds. Place 1 inch apart on a greased cookie sheet. Bake for 20 minutes or until golden brown. Allow to cool. The cookies can be stored in an airtight container for up to 1 week.

Zabaglione

This is the most famous of Italian-American desserts. There are so many things you can do with *zabaglione*: put it on top of a piece of pound cake; jazz up your favorite ice cream with a dollop of it; or serve it the classic way with fresh berries. It's also great with any kind of fresh or poached fruit. You can serve it right away or allow it to cool and fold in some whipped cream to make a marvelous mousse.

Serves 6

10 egg yolks (use extra-large eggs)
1 cup sugar
1 cup dry marsala wine

Fill a large pot halfway with water and bring to a boil. Reduce the heat to a very low simmer.

Place the egg yolks, sugar, and marsala in a large stainless steel bowl. Place the bowl over the pot of simmering water. (Do not let the bottom of the bowl touch the water; you can also use a double boiler.) Continuously whisk the egg mixture until it triples in volume and holds a figure eight when the whisk is removed, about 4 to 6 minutes.

Serve warm or cold.

Sicilian Oranges

Sicily produces some of the best citrus fruit in the world, particularly oranges. The original Sicilian version of this recipe probably called for blood oranges, but you can use regular oranges as well. If you can't find good, ripe, sweet oranges, forget about it. Just wait until they're available. And whatever you do, don't substitute grapefruit. They're too sour.

Serves 6

⅔ cup shredded coconut
6 large navel or blood oranges
1¾ cups sugar
pinch of ground cloves

Preheat the oven to 375° F.

Spread the coconut over a cookie sheet and bake until nicely browned.

Remove the pith and peel of the oranges with a paring knife. Julienne the orange peels. Bring 4 cups water to a boil in a small saucepan. Add the julienned orange peels and boil for about 5 minutes. Reserve ⅓ cup of the liquid and the peels.

In a skillet, combine the sugar, the reserved orange water, and ground cloves. Bring the liquid to a boil and allow to cook until it turns a rich amber color. (Do not let the liquid get too dark; it will continue to cook after it is removed from the heat and will taste burnt.) Remove from the heat and carefully add the peel. Set aside and allow to cool.

Remove any remaining pith from the oranges and cut them into 6 slices each. Place in a pyrex dish, top with the syrup, and sprinkle with the toasted coconut.

Refrigerate for at least 2 hours before serving.

Tegole d'Aosta

CHOCOLATE-COVERED AMARETTO-HAZELNUT COOKIES

Aosta is a town in the north of Italy, tucked up against the Alps, so of course they have quite a lot of snow during the winter. Many of the houses have the old-style pitched roofs with big shingles, which are called *tegole*. The cookies from that area look like those shingles and hence the name.

Makes about 2 dozen

5 tablespoons butter, at room temperature

$\frac{1}{2}$ cup granulated sugar

1 tablespoon vanilla extract

1 tablespoon grated lemon zest

$\frac{2}{3}$ cup ground hazelnuts

$\frac{1}{2}$ cup amaretto cookie crumbs (see page 173)

3 tablespoons flour

2 egg whites

1 cup confectioners' sugar

1 ounce semisweet chocolate, chopped

Preheat the oven to 375° F.

In a large bowl, beat together the butter, granulated sugar, vanilla, and lemon zest until smooth.

In another bowl, combine the hazelnuts, cookie crumbs, and flour. Fold into the butter mixture.

Whip the egg whites until they form stiff peaks. Gently fold the whites into the other ingredients with a spatula.

Spoon teaspoonfuls of dough onto a greased cookie sheet. Flatten and shape the mounds into circles with the back of a spoon. Bake for 6 minutes, until golden brown.

Remove the cookies carefully from the cookie sheet with a metal spatula while they are still hot. Lay the cookies on a rolling pin to shape them into curves. Allow the cookies to cool on the pin, about 1 minute.

In a saucepan, bring $\frac{1}{4}$ cup water to a boil. Add the powdered sugar and the chocolate. Stir until the glaze is smooth. Reserve.

Once cooled, spoon the glaze over the cookies and serve.

A bounty of assorted hand-made fruit marzipan

Alba's Italian Pastry Shoppe

Artistry in Sugar and Cream

If you didn't know any better, you'd think the shiny fruit in the display case at Alba's Pastry Shop on 18th Avenue at 70th Street in the Bensonhurst section of Brooklyn were perfect little hand-painted wooden sculptures, marvels of handicraft representing apples, figs, bananas, strawberries. They're not. They're marzipan, a Sicilian specialty and truly one of the sweetest, most delicious treats you'll ever put in your mouth.

"Marzipan is a special holiday favorite. Basically, it's like a raw macaroon," says Sal Alba, the manager who's worked at the shop since 1932 when it was his father's business. "You take the almonds, blanch them, powder them, mix them with a little corn syrup to get the right consistency and then sculpt them. They have a very long shelf life, although they do harden up after a while."

Luigi DiRosa, the head pastry chef and general supervisor, is Sal Alba's nephew. Luigi comes from Aidone in the province of Enna, Sicily. He stays in touch with his roots by taking yearly cruises around the Mediterranean as well as trips back to Sicily as often as his demanding schedule at the pastry shop allows.

"Our biggest-selling item is the cannoli," he says. "We use about 100 pounds of flour a week to make about 2,000 cannoli. In the busy season—that's September, October, November—we probably make 60 wedding cakes a week." They also make *sfogliatelle*, all kinds of biscotti,

Luigi DiRosa

macaroons, and, of course, a superb cheesecake—over 250 varieties of pastry that are a feast for the eyes as well as the stomach.

In 1919, Nicolo and Adele Alba came to New York from their birthplace of Caltigirone, Sicily. The next year, their son Sal was born. Two daughters, Ann and Bianca, followed. In 1932, with vision, determination, and plenty of traditional pastry recipes, they opened their shop at 7001 18th Avenue, Brooklyn. Often they were open 12 hours a day, 7 days a week. Eventually, the business expanded to employ four generations of Albas as well as many people from the neighborhood and from the Old Country. Nicolo passed away in 1948, but his children have kept the business going on the same spot.

Alba's mail-order business sends cheesecake all over the world. And Brooklyn residents who've migrated far and wide still come back to the old pastry shop to savor a taste of the Old World and satisfy their sweet tooth.

Chapter Eight

Amici

Friends are sacred to Italian-Americans. As a kid, my grandfather always told me that you measured a person's wealth not by how much money he had, but how many friends he had. Now, true friends are hard to come by. A handful is a lot. I am lucky that I have some very good friends, people I'd do anything for without hesitation. I want to dedicate this chapter to the greatest friend anyone could have, Danny. He is not only a great person and an inspiration, but he's also a great cook. He has a creed that anyone learns the minute they meet him: Don't put onion and garlic into the same tomato sauce. This one is for you, Danny.

Anna Nurse's Baked Smoked Ham

1 large smoked ham, about 12 to 18 pounds

whole cloves

3 cups pineapple juice

1 pound dark brown sugar

1 16-ounce bottle dark corn syrup

Here is one of the most famous ham recipes anywhere, from Anna Amendolara Nurse, a truly lovely lady, generous and kind, and one of the greatest cooking teachers of all time.

You might not think of this as a particularly Italian-American recipe, but it is—maybe with an emphasis on the American. As Anna says, even at a traditional Italian-American Christmas this ham is always on the sideboard: "It may not be the main feature, but it's always an extra added attraction." When you put away all the perishable foods, the pies stay out and the ham stays out, ready for snacking at any time.

This ham has been the centerpiece of the James Beard Foundation fundraiser brunches that Anna has run for the last ten years. This recipe has also appeared in print many times, and there's a reason for that: It's the best! Anna uses Lundy smoked country hams from North Carolina because she likes their consistency—they're never too salty, never too fatty.

Serves 8 to 12 as a main dish, lunch, or snack

Preheat the oven to 325° F.

Place the ham in a shallow roasting pan. Score the fat and stud it completely with cloves. Pour the pineapple juice over the ham and bake for 12 minutes per pound.

After $1\frac{1}{2}$ hours, remove the ham from the oven and carefully pat the brown sugar on top, completely covering the top of the ham. Gently pour the corn syrup over the ham, being careful not to disturb the sugar covering. Continue baking, basting every 15 minutes.

When the ham has baked its allotted time, remove it from oven and continue basting until it is cooled—this gives it a beautiful glaze. The remaining syrup can be used again over a side dish such as yams, butternut squash, or sweet potatoes if you are serving the ham hot as a main dish. Otherwise, it can be left on the sideboard or kitchen counter at room temperature during the day for snacking purposes, then stored in the refrigerator for several days.

Festa Meat Salad

This recipe is courtesy of my good friend Dominick Di Napoli, an excellent young cook who worked for me at my restaurant, Nonna. This is one of the classic dishes you might find at a good *salumeria*, pork store, or Italian deli-grocery. It makes use of some of the best products of that store. It's a welcome addition to a summer picnic or back-yard celebration, and to any antipasto plate. Make sure to have some good crusty Italian bread on hand to go with it.

Serves 6 as an appetizer, main dish, or snack

¼ pound hard Genoa salami

¼ pound pepperoni

¼ pound mortadella

¼ pound sweet or hot ham

¼ pound provolone

3 large artichoke hearts

1 large roasted pepper

½ cup green olives, pitted

½ cup black olives, pitted

1 teaspoon dried oregano

1 teaspoon crushed red pepper flakes

½ cup red wine vinegar

¾ cup extra virgin olive oil

salt and pepper to taste

Slice the cold cuts and cheese into thick slices, then cut into medium-size cubes. There should be about 1 cup of each.

Cut the artichoke hearts into four pieces, or if they are very large, into six pieces.

Cut the roasted pepper into large strips. Cut the olives into small rings.

In a large bowl mix together all the ingredients. Let stand in the refrigerator for 1 day before serving. This salad can become a staple of your *antipasto* platter; it also keeps very well in the fridge for up to 1 week. Most people will agree it's actually better the second day.

Joey "Bats" Cannelloni

Joey "Bats" is one of my best friends. He lives on Eighth Avenue in Brooklyn. I'm sure your first question is not about the cannelloni, but why we call him "Bats." I wish I could say it's because he's a good baseball player, but the real reason is that he's a little crazy. Joey is also a great cook, although he'd never admit it in public. One of his best recipes is this cannelloni. You can make them ahead and freeze them if you like.

Serves 4 as a first course or main dish

½ pound ricotta cheese

4 ounces fresh mozzarella cheese, shredded

3 ounces prosciutto, finely diced

1 egg

2 tablespoons chopped fresh Italian parsley

¼ cup grated Parmesan cheese

salt and pepper to taste

½ pound pasta dough (see Basic Recipes, page 218), rolled into 10 sheets, each 5 x 5 inches, and ¹⁄₁₆-inch thick

1½ cups Garden Tomato Sauce (see Basic Recipes, page 217)

In a bowl, combine the ricotta, mozzarella, prosciutto, egg, parsley, and half the Parmesan cheese. Season with salt and pepper, mix well, and set aside.

Lightly oil a small baking dish and set aside. Preheat the oven to 375° F.

Bring a large pot of salted water to a rolling boil over high heat. Have a bowl of ice water ready on the side. Precook the pasta, 4 sheets at a time, for 40 seconds, refreshing in the ice water afterwards. Repeat until all the pasta is cooked. Remove the pasta from the ice water and lay flat on damp towels to drain. Spoon 2 generous tablespoons of the filling mixture down the center of each pasta sheet and roll it up so it looks like a big, fat cigar. Arrange the cannelloni in the baking dish, side by side. Spoon the tomato sauce on top and sprinkle with the remaining Parmesan. Bake the cannelloni for 20 minutes, until the cheese is melted and bubbling. Remove carefully to warm plates, spoon the sauce around the plates, and serve immediately.

Fusilli with Joe's Spicy Tomato Sauce

Joe Radarazzo is an old friend who is a wonderful cook. He is also the Italian Felix Unger. He tiled his backyard and carpeted his garage. He even put aluminum siding on the dog house! In the kitchen, Joe is a meticulous cook who insists on taking the sausage meat out of the casing. Most similar recipes don't bother with this step, but I think it's a nice touch.

Serves 4 as a first course or main dish

2 tablespoons olive oil

3 cloves garlic, chopped

½ pound sweet Italian sausage, casing removed, crumbled

1 16-ounce can peeled plum tomatoes, seeded and diced

1 pepperoncini, seeded and diced

1 pound fusilli

⅔ cup grated Parmesan cheese

1 tablespoon chopped fresh Italian parsley

½ teaspoon salt

In a sauté pan, heat the olive oil over medium heat. Add the garlic and sauté until it turns golden brown. (Do not let the garlic burn or it will taste bitter.) Lower the heat and add the crumbled sausages. Cook for about 3 minutes. Add the tomatoes and the pepperoncini and continue to cook for 10 minutes more. Cook the pasta according to the instructions on the package. Mix the cheese, parsley, and salt into the sauce. Toss the cooked pasta with the sauce and serve.

Cousin Vinny's Linguine with Scallops

Like most Italian families, mine has a Cousin Vinny. Except *my* Cousin Vinny is a terrific cook. Every Fourth of July, we have a huge barbecue and everyone brings something. One of my favorite dishes is Vinny's linguine with scallop sauce.

Serves 6 to 8 as a first course or main dish

6 tablespoons olive oil

4 cloves garlic, minced

2 shallots, minced

5 fresh basil leaves, chopped

1/2 teaspoon crushed red pepper flakes

2 teaspoons chopped fresh Italian parsley

1/2 teaspoon fresh thyme leaves

2 28-ounce cans peeled plum tomatoes

1/2 cup dry white wine

1 pound white mushrooms, washed and sliced

1 pound linguine

2 pounds bay scallops

1 tablespoon lemon juice

1/2 teaspoon freshly ground black pepper

Heat 2 tablespoons of the olive oil in a large saucepan over medium heat. Add the garlic and shallots and sauté for 3 minutes, until golden brown. Add the basil, pepper flakes, parsley, thyme, tomatoes, and wine. Bring to a boil. Lower the heat and simmer for 20 minutes, then add mushrooms.

Cook the pasta al dente according to the instructions on the package.

Heat the remaining 4 tablespoons of olive oil in a skillet over high heat. Add the scallops and quickly sauté for 1 minute. Add the lemon juice and pepper. Add the scallops to the sauce, spoon immediately over the linguine, and serve.

Mamma Salerno's Panzarotti

POTATO CROQUETTES

Mamma Salerno was my friend Charlie's great grandmother. She's been gone for a few years, but I have fond memories of these tasty snacks she used to make for us. They are a kind of stuffed potato croquette that can be prepared up to two days in advance, then fried at the last minute. You can have fun with the filling, too, adding prosciutto, peas, shrimp, or whatever you think will taste good.

Serves 8 as an appetizer or snack

Sauce

¼ cup extra virgin olive oil

2 tablespoons chopped garlic

1 shallot, minced

1 teaspoon crushed red pepper flakes

3 tomatoes, peeled, seeded, and chopped

Croquettes

4 large Idaho potatoes, peeled

3 egg yolks

½ cup grated Parmesan cheese

1 teaspoon salt

1 teaspoon pepper

¼ pound mozzarella cheese, cut into ¼-inch dice

3 egg whites, slightly beaten until frothy

1½ cups breadcrumbs

vegetable oil for frying

To make the sauce: Heat the olive oil in a small pan over medium heat. Add the garlic and sauté until beige. Add the shallot and cook until translucent and the garlic is a light golden color. (Don't let the garlic burn or it will taste bitter.) Add the pepper flakes and sauté for about 10 seconds more. Add the tomatoes and simmer for 15 to 20 minutes.

To make the croquettes: Preheat the oven to 200° F.

In a saucepan, boil the potatoes until tender. Drain the potatoes, place on a sheet pan, and allow to dry in the oven for about 5 to 10 minutes. Pass the potatoes through a food mill or ricer *(passatutto)* and let them cool in a bowl. Stir in the egg yolks and the Parmesan cheese. Season with the salt and pepper.

Place 2 tablespoons of the potato mixture in the palm of your hand and make a small ball. Make an indentation in the center with your thumb. Place 3 cubes of the mozzarella in the center and bring up the sides of the potato mixture to cover it. Pinch it well and then roll it between the palms of your hands until it forms a stick about 2½ inches long. Repeat the process. Once you have all the potato sticks done, roll them in the egg whites, then in the breadcrumbs. Remove excess crumbs and again roll them lightly between the palms of your hands to set the breadcrumbs.

Pour vegetable oil to a depth of 2 inches into a skillet and heat until a drop of batter dropped into the oil rises right away. Deep fry the croquettes until golden brown, drain on paper towels, and serve immediately with the sauce on the side for dipping.

Joey "Lips" Sausage and Ricotta Pie

Italian-Americans have a habit of making a pie out of everything. My grandmother makes zucchini pie, grain pie, cauliflower pie, or pie from anything she has left in the refrigerator. This recipe is from the house of a friend of mine, Joey. It isn't Joey's recipe, it's his wife Lena's. But it comes from his home and Joey takes credit for it.

Serves 8 as a first course, main dish, or snack

4 pounds sweet Italian sausage, casing removed

4 eggs

3 cups ricotta cheese

1 pound mozzarella cheese, shredded

½ cup chopped fresh Italian parsley leaves

⅛ teaspoon white pepper

1 pie crust (see Basic Recipes, page 218)

4 hard-boiled eggs, peeled and thinly sliced

In a skillet over medium heat, sauté the sausage meat until browned, about 4 minutes. Pour off the excess fat, place the meat in a bowl, and allow to cool. Then add 3 of the eggs, the cheeses, parsley, and white pepper.

Preheat the oven to 350° F.

Divide the pie crust dough in half and roll each piece into a circle ⅛-inch thick. Line an 8-inch springform pan with half the dough. Pour the filling into the pan and then lay the hard-boiled eggs on top of the filling. Lay the remaining dough on top, and with a small knife trim off the excess. Fold the edges of the crust over the rim, seal and pinch the crusts together. Cut a few slits for steam vents on the top. Mix the remaining egg with 1 tablespoon of water and brush the top of the pie with it.

Bake for 40 minutes, until golden brown. Remove from the oven and cut into eighths; serve hot, or allow to cool, cut into smaller pieces, and serve at room temperature as an appetizer or snack. Store the leftovers in the fridge and serve any time of day.

Pollo al Mattone

PIERO'S CHICKEN COOKED WITH A BRICK

Piero was the neighborhood undertaker where I grew up. I remember him as a morbid character who was also a great cook. When Piero's beloved wife Rosalie died, he embalmed her and put her in a glass case in the living room. He would change her clothes on special occasions. Everybody in the neighborhood thought he was *pazzo*—crazy. Then he met a hot young tomato named Maria. Poor Rosalie moved to the garage and she never got a change of clothes again!

He had a delicious way of preparing chicken—marinating it with herbs, browning the skin, then finishing it in the oven. The earthenware brick, called a *mattone*, helps it cook fast and hot so it becomes wonderfully crispy. This dish goes particularly well with a salad of seasonal greens or arugula.

Serves 2 as a main course

1 3-pound chicken, split in the back with the rib bones removed

5 cloves garlic, sliced in half

1 sprig fresh marjoram, leaves only

1 sprig fresh basil, leaves only, julienned

4 tablespoons olive oil

juice of 1 lemon

salt and coarsely cracked pepper

1 *mattone*—an earthenware brick used in Italy; if not available, use a plain brick wrapped in aluminum foil

Preheat the oven to 450° F. Preheat the *mattone*.

Place the chicken in a bowl with the garlic, marjoram, basil, 3 tablespoons of the olive oil, lemon juice, and season with salt and pepper. Refrigerate and allow to marinate for 2 to 3 hours.

Heat the remaining tablespoon of olive oil in a heavy, ovenproof skillet over medium heat. Remove the chicken from the bowl, leaving the garlic cloves but allowing a sufficient amount of herbs to cling to the chicken. Place the bird skin-side down in the skillet and cook for 3 minutes. Remove from heat. Place the *mattone* on top of the chicken in a roasting pan and bake for 20 minutes.

Remove the roasting pan from the oven, remove the *mattone*, and turn the chicken over. Cook for 3 more minutes in the skillet on top of the stove, remove to warm plates, and serve.

Mamma Palumbo's Egg Croquettes

Every Friday night when I was a kid we used to go to the Palumbos' house on 79th Street in Bay Ridge to watch the older guys play the Italian card game *ziganette*. The grandmother, Mamma Palumbo, used to make a lot of snacks. The hands-down favorite was always her Egg Croquettes.

Serves 4 as an appetizer, first course, snack, or main dish

4 eggs, beaten

½ cup fresh breadcrumbs

⅔ cup grated Parmesan cheese

5 tablespoons chopped fresh Italian parsley

3 tablespoons olive oil

1 onion, chopped

2 cloves garlic, finely minced

1 cup Garden Tomato Sauce (see Basic Recipes, page 217)

½ cup chicken stock (see Basic Recipes, page 216)

1 cup frozen peas

1 cup long-grain rice, cooked in 2 cups of chicken stock

In a bowl, combine the eggs, breadcrumbs, cheese, and parsley. Using a soup spoon, form the mixture into dumplings. They should be about 1½ tablespoons each, thick, short cigar-width cylinders. Set aside.

Heat the olive oil in a saucepan over medium heat and sauté the onion and garlic for 2 minutes; do not allow the garlic to brown. Add the tomato sauce and chicken stock and bring to a simmer. Gently spoon the dumplings and the peas into the sauce, cover, and lower the heat. Allow to simmer for 30 minutes. Do not stir because the dumplings are very delicate. Remove from the pan gently and serve in bowls over the rice with the sauce spooned on top.

Pasta Lentiche

PASTA WITH LENTILS

I include this recipe in honor of George, one of my closest friends and family members. George is very traditional, and a great storyteller. One of his funniest stories is about a restaurant he frequents, which, by the way, is not Italian. He tried to explain to the chef that he wanted one of the most popular and basic dishes to us Southern Italians, *Pasta Lentiche*, Pasta with Lentils. It is a simple dish using small green lentils and a short cut of pasta, like ditali. This poor chef caught George's wrath because, not only did he not use the small lentils, but he made the dish with long ziti and then made George wait while he cut them with a pair of scissors!

Serves 4 to 6 as a first course or main dish

2 cups pre-rinsed small green lentils, preferably Italian or French

1 large carrot, peeled and cut into ¼-inch dice

1 small red onion, finely chopped

1 stalk celery, cut into ¼-inch dice

1 small clove garlic, peeled and left whole

1 teaspoon salt

6 cups water or chicken stock (see Basic Recipes, page 216)

1 cup ditali or other small pasta, such as rotini

freshly ground black pepper to taste

¼ cup extra virgin olive oil

2 tablespoons chopped fresh Italian parsley

pecorino cheese, grated

In a deep saucepan, combine the lentils, carrot, onion, celery, garlic, salt, and the water or chicken stock. Bring to a boil over medium heat. Reduce the heat, cover, and simmer for 25 minutes or until the vegetables are barely tender. Don't overcook. Remove from the heat, remove the garlic clove, and set aside.

Cook the pasta until al dente according to the instructions on the package. Drain and add to the lentil mixture. Mix well and add some fresh pepper. Drizzle with the olive oil, sprinkle with the parsley, and serve with grated cheese sprinkled on top.

Zia Maria's Onion and Egg Soup

I think my Aunt Maria was the original "Frugal Gourmet." I'm not saying she was cheap, just that she could do amazing things with very little. This is a classic example of her ingenuity in the kitchen. Even though she's family, I've included her recipe in this chapter on friends, because she's a friend, too.

Serves 4 as a first course

¼ pound unsalted butter

3 large onions, thinly sliced

2 tablespoons flour

1½ quarts chicken stock (see Basic Recipes, page 216)

½ teaspoon salt

4 egg yolks

½ cup grated Parmesan cheese

8 slices Italian bread, toasted

In a heavy-bottomed soup pot, melt the butter over medium heat. Add the onions and sauté until translucent, about 6 minutes. Sprinkle the flour over and mix well, cooking for an additional 2 minutes. Add the chicken stock and mix well. Bring to a boil, then reduce the heat to low and

allow to simmer for 8 minutes. In a bowl, whisk together the salt, egg yolks, and cheese. Whisk the egg mixture into the soup. Allow to cook for 2 minutes. Place 2 slices of bread in each soup bowl, ladle the soup on top, and serve.

Zampino

STUFFED PIG'S FOOT WITH BRAISED SAVOY CABBAGE

My good friend Marc Bussio owns Manhattan's Salumeria Biellese, which produces some of the best pork specialties, both Italian and French. He makes superior domestic prosciutto, salami, sausages, and one of my favorites, *Zampino di Modena*. *Zampino* is a fantastic, garlic-flavored stuffed pig's foot, a rare delicacy that can be hard to find but is definitely worth the effort.

Serves 6 as a main dish

4 pounds stuffed *zampino*

1 large onion

3 whole cloves

1 large carrot, peeled and chopped into ¹/₂-inch pieces

2 celery stalks, chopped into ¹/₂-inch pieces

3 cloves garlic

1 tablespoon salt

Garnish

2 heads savoy cabbage

2 tablespoons butter

1 large onion, halved then sliced into ¹/₄-inch wedges

¹/₄ cup bacon-slab, cut into ¹/₄-inch cubes

1 apple, halved, cored, and sliced (unpeeled)

6 cups chicken stock (see Basic Recipes, page 216)

2 teaspoons salt

¹/₂ teaspoon pepper

With the top of a small paring knife, poke 6 to 8 small holes into the *zampino* skin. Wrap the *zampino* well in a doubled cheesecloth and tie it tightly with string. Place the *zampino* in a large stock pot. Stud the onion with the cloves and place in the pot with the *zampino*. Add the carrot, celery, garlic, salt, and water to cover. Bring to a boil and then immediately lower the heat to a simmer for 1 hour. (Do not let the water continue to boil or the *zampino* skin will burst open.)

Preheat the oven to 400° F.

After 1 hour, remove the *zampino*. Carefully transfer it to a lightly oiled roasting pan and bake until the skin is golden brown, about 20 minutes. Turn the *zampino* occasionally to brown on all sides. Be careful not to rip the skin when turning. While the *zampino* is cooking, prepare the garnish as follows. (If the *zampino* is done and you're still working on the garnish, simply take it out of the oven and leave it on a warm platter covered with a warm, wet towel.)

Remove the outer leaves, cores, and ribs from the cabbages. Cut into 2-inch chunks.

In a large stockpot, heat 2 quarts of salted water until it comes to a boil. Blanch the cabbage in the boiling water. Drain in a large colander and run cold water over it until it cools. Set aside.

Heat the butter in a large, ovenproof pot. Add the onion and sauté over low heat until wilted and brown. Add the bacon and cook 3 to 4 minutes. Add the apple, cabbage, and chicken stock. Season with the salt and pepper. Cover and bake in the oven for 30 minutes or until the cabbage is completely softened. Arrange the vegetables around a warm platter, put the *zampino* in the middle and serve everything hot. *Zampino* can be refrigerated for several days and is great as a leftover.

Tortellini alla Danny

Danny and I both come from Brooklyn and we're great friends, even though he's 20 years older. I have learned a lot from Danny, especially about cooking. This recipe is for a pasta salad he makes that can stand alone as a meal in itself. It calls for cheese tortellini, which are the delicious little donut-shaped stuffed pastas; make sure you use the cheese-stuffed ones, not the meat ones.

Serves 4 as an appetizer, side dish, snack, or main dish

1 pound cheese tortellini

**4 medium zucchini, washed and sliced
  ¼-inch thick**

vegetable oil for deep frying

¼ cup olive oil

4 cloves garlic, sliced

¼ cup fresh mint, julienned

¼ cup Chianti or red wine vinegar

1 teaspoon cracked black pepper

¾ teaspoon salt

Cook the pasta according to the instructions on the package. Drain and reserve.

Dry the zucchini on paper towels. Place vegetable oil in a deep fryer or large pot to a depth of 2 inches and heat oil until it's very hot (at the smoking point). Fry one quarter of the zucchini until it turns golden brown. Drain on paper towels. Repeat until all the zucchini is fried.

Heat the olive oil in a skillet over medium heat. Add the garlic and sauté until it starts to color. Remove from the heat, add the mint and vinegar. Toss the mixture in the skillet with the zucchini. Mix in the pasta and season with the pepper and salt. Allow to cool to room temperature before serving. Refrigerate the leftovers, but let them come back to room temperature before serving again.

Totonno's Pizzeria Napolitano

They Make It the Old-Fashioned Way

At Totonno's Pizzeria, 1524 Neptune Avenue, Coney Island, Brooklyn, they've been making pizza the same way on the same spot since 1924. Totonno Pero, who immigrated from Naples, was 17 years old when he went to work as a pizza chef at Gennaro Lombardi's pizzeria at 53½ Spring Street, Manhattan, in 1905. Some say that was the first pizzeria in America—maybe the first anywhere. There's a photo on the wall at Totonno's showing the young chef and his boss on the doorstep of the shop.

Totonno's granddaughter, Louise Ciminieri, and her husband Joel, run the place now. Their son Lawrence, representing the fourth generation, makes the dough. Joel is the pizza chef. The co-owners are two other grandchildren of Totonno, which, by the way, is short for Antonio: Louise's sister and brother, Antoinette Bencivenga and Frank Balzano.

For many years, the famous Jerry Pero presided at Totonno's. Jerry was Totonno's son. He only made a certain amount of dough each day. And when that dough ran out, he would announce the predicament to his customers in no uncertain terms, usually something to the effect of "Okay, everybody out! No more dough." That meant *everybody*, even loyal customers who'd been waiting in line for an hour and a half. Needless to say,

Joel Ciminieri (above); Louise Ciminieri (right)

Jerry was one of New York's all-time great Italian-American characters. Those customers kept coming back, and they still do, even though Jerry passed away in 1994.

"Jerry was smart," Joel says. "I was in the auto business when he talked me into joining him. He had me convinced I was going to be the maitre'd, you know, greeting people at the door and showing them to their tables. Little did I know what he had planned for me—to be the pizza maker some day."

The secret of Totonno's pies is their crisp, light dough, and the freshness of the ingredients. The dough is still made every day, only for that day, although now they have enough for everybody. It is unrefrigerated and it tastes better than most Italian breads. The mozzarella is also made fresh daily and sliced painstakingly by hand. Joel puts the cheese on the dough, with the tomato sauce on top, so the sauce doesn't soak into the crust and make it soggy. The pizza cooks in Totonno's brick, coal-burning oven at 875°F. for about 6 minutes. It's some of the lightest, freshest pizza you'll ever taste: a unique taste from a unique institution.

Basic Recipes

Bagna Cauda

Bagna cauda in Latin, or *bagna caldo* in Italian, means "hot bath." It is a delicious dip that makes a wonderful accompaniment to fish, boiled meats, and especially vegetables. It is easy to make and a quick solution for last-minute meals.

Makes about 1 cup

1 cup extra virgin olive oil
4 cloves garlic, finely chopped
6 anchovy fillets, rinsed and chopped
pinch of crushed red pepper flakes
freshly ground black pepper
1 tablespoon chopped fresh Italian parsley

Heat the olive oil and the garlic in a double boiler over medium heat for 8 to 10 minutes, or until the oil is hot. Turn off the heat but leave the pot on the stove. Add the anchovies, pepper flakes, and pepper; keep warm for 20 minutes, allowing the flavors to combine thoroughly. Add the parsley and serve.

Candied Fruit Peels

This recipe can be made with either lemon or orange peels, or both.

Makes about 1/2 cup

peel of 1 orange
peel of 1 lemon
1/2 cup sugar

Blanch the peels in boiling water. Refresh in an ice bath and repeat. In a saucepan, dissolve the sugar in 1/2 cup of water. Boil until thick and syrupy, about 4 to 5 minutes. Add the peels and cook for 5 minutes. Remove the peels from the liquid and allow to cool. They are ready to use for desserts and garnishes.

Chicken Stock

Makes about 2 quarts

4 chicken carcasses, excess fat and skin removed
1 stalk celery
1 small onion, quartered
1 clove garlic
1 small carrot, cut into 4 pieces
1 bay leaf
1 sprig fresh thyme
1/4 teaspoon whole peppercorns

Place all the ingredients in a soup pot and cover with about 4 quarts cold water. Bring to a boil over high heat, lower the heat, and simmer for 1 hour, periodically skimming the excess fat from the top of the stock. Pass through a fine strainer and allow to cool to room temperature before refrigerating. The stock can be frozen in plastic containers or ice cube trays for up to 3 months.

Herbed Olive Oil

Makes about 1 cup

1 cup fresh herbs, picked clean (basil, Italian parsley, chives)

1 cup extra virgin olive oil

Blanch the herbs in salted boiling water for 30 seconds and refresh in ice water. Remove from ice water and squeeze dry. Place in a blender and add the olive oil. Process until the herbs are pureed.

Store the oil in the refrigerator unless you are going to use it within a few hours. The oil can stand up to one week.

Garden Tomato Sauce

When you make this sauce for future use, it is very important to let it cool to room temperature before refrigerating it. Put it in plastic containers, and freeze it for up to 3 months. It can also be kept in the refrigerator for up to 4 days.

Makes about 2 cups

¼ cup extra virgin olive oil

4 cloves garlic, chopped

pinch of crushed red pepper flakes

8 cups diced, peeled, and seeded plum tomatoes

1½ teaspoons salt

¼ teaspoon pepper

3 tablespoons chopped fresh basil

Heat the olive oil in a saucepan over medium heat. Add the garlic and sauté until golden brown. Add the pepper flakes and cook for 1 minute. Stir in the tomatoes, season with the salt and pepper, and cook, partially covered, over low heat for 25 minutes. Add the basil when the sauce is almost completely cooked.

Pizza Dough

Makes about 6 12-inch pizza crusts

1 tablespoon water

¼ teaspoon sugar

¼ teaspoon yeast

3¼ pounds (13 cups) bread flour or all-purpose flour

1 quart water at 90° F.

2 tablespoons olive oil

1 egg

1 tablespoon salt

Mix 1 tablespoon of the water, the sugar, and ⅛ teaspoon of the yeast in a small bowl.

Place one third of the flour in the mixing bowl of a mixer fitted with the hook attachment. Add the warm water, olive oil, dissolved yeast, egg, and salt and mix for 5 minutes on low speed. Fold in another third of the flour and continue to mix for another 5 minutes on slow speed. Add the remaining flour and the remaining ⅛ teaspoon of dry yeast, increase the speed to medium, and continue to mix for an additional 5 minutes.

Place the dough in a lightly oiled bowl, cover with plastic wrap, and allow to rest in the refrigerator for 1 hour.

Divide the dough into 6 7-inch circles, approximately 4 ounces each. Rub your hands with a little oil so the dough won't stick to your fingers. Place the dough on a lightly oiled cookie sheet, cover well with plastic wrap, and let them rest in a warm place for another 3 hours.

Flatten and form the dough into 12-inch circles, add the desired toppings, and bake according to the recipe. The dough can be wrapped in individual-pizza portions and refrigerated for up to 5 days, or it can be frozen.

Place the two flours into the bowl of an electric mixer or food processor, attach the paddle, and start the motor slowly. Add the eggs 1 at a time, waiting 2 minutes between each egg. The dough may appear to be too lumpy, so continue to process until all the ingredients are well incorporated. Stop the machine, remove the dough to a floured work surface, and knead for 3 minutes. If the dough is too sticky you can add a little more flour. Wrap the dough in plastic wrap and refrigerate until ready to roll. If you are making the dough for future use, dust it with a little durum flour and store it in the fridge for about 3 days or in the freezer for up to 3 months.

Once you've prepared the dough and are ready to make the pasta shapes, you can do it either by using a pasta cutting machine or by rolling it out by hand with a rolling pin and cutting into the desired shapes.

To make spinach pasta: Blanch in boiling water, cool, squeeze dry, and finely chop enough spinach to fill 1 cup. Thoroughly combine the spinach with the flours in the mixer before starting to add the eggs.

Pasta Dough

Makes 1½ pounds of dough

2 cups unbleached all-purpose flour

2 cups durum wheat flour

5 eggs

Pie Crust

Makes 1 8-inch single-crust pie

3 eggs

2 tablespoons vegetable oil

2 tablespoons water

2 cups flour

1 teaspoon baking powder

In a bowl, beat together the eggs, oil, and water and set aside. Sift together the flour and the baking powder into a large mixing bowl. Make a well in the center of the flour and slowly add the egg mixture, blending it with the flour. Mix until it forms a ball but not beyond that point. Cover and set aside for 10 minutes.

Polenta

Although I am an advocate of instant polenta, which I feel makes the home cook's life a lot easier and is just as good as the real thing, here's the traditional way to make it, just like my grandmother does.

Serves 4 to 6

5 cups water or chicken stock (see page 216)
2 teaspoons salt
1 pound (4 cups) yellow cornmeal
¼ cup grated Parmesan cheese
3 tablespoons unsalted butter

Heat the water or chicken stock in a saucepan over high heat. Bring to a boil, add the salt, reduce the heat to low, and slowly pour the cornmeal into the boiling water. Stir constantly with a wooden spoon for about 20 to 30 minutes, or until the cornmeal leaves the side of the pot easily. Add the cheese and butter, stir until well-incorporated, and serve.

Seasoned Breadcrumbs

For this recipe, you will need some stale Italian bread; make sure it's really stale and hard because otherwise it won't work. These breadcrumbs are an essential ingredient for stuffings, coatings for fried foods, and sprinkling on and in casseroles.

Makes 1 cup

1 cup stale Italian bread, cut into ½-inch cubes
1 teaspoon chopped fresh Italian parsley
¼ teaspoon chopped fresh basil
¼ teaspoon chopped fresh oregano
⅛ teaspoon salt
1 tablespoon grated pecorino cheese
freshly ground black pepper to taste

Trim the crusts off the bread, then grate it by hand or with the grating attachment of a food processor into a bowl. Mix well with all the other ingredients.

Tips and Fundamentals

Anchovies

Always rinse anchovy fillets in water after you take them out of the can or jar. This takes away the excess saltiness.

Canned tomatoes

Look for genuine "San Marzano" tomatoes, which are not a brand but a type of tomato grown near Naples—they are the sweetest, meatiest kind. Look for *pelati*, that is peeled, plum tomatoes. Don't discard the juice from the can, particularly when the recipe calls for a long cooking time. It will thicken up and add to your sauce.

Fresh Tomatoes

Look for the ones that still have the stem on top. The greenness of the stem reveals the freshness of the tomato. It should be fragrant at the stem. Avoid green tomatoes; even though they will ripen at room temperature, they will be mealy and mushy.

A word about fresh versus canned tomatoes: Whenever you find very fresh, very ripe, very tasty plum tomatoes, use them. Unfortunately, this is only for a couple of months of the year, depending on where you live. In the off months, opt for a can of San Marzano tomatoes. They're better than fresh ones that aren't ripe and won't ever ripen properly off the vine. You should always use the freshest, best ingredients possible. In the case of tomatoes, fresh is only best when they're ripe.

Chopping Onions

I teach a lot of cooking classes and I'm frequently asked how to chop an onion without shedding a tear. When you cut an onion, you're cutting through the onion's cells, releasing juices and particles that cause a reaction with the moisture in your eyes. To prevent this, simply chill the onion. Cutting the root end will also help.

Eggplant

Whether you slice it or cube it, always be sure to salt the eggplant well and let it sit in a colander for about an hour before cooking. This draws the excess moisture out of it. Pat the eggplant pieces dry and they're ready to use.

Garlic

To store peeled garlic cloves for a long period of time, soak them in white vinegar for 12 hours and then store them in a good olive oil. The vinegar will reduce the chance of contamination. After you use that last piece of garlic, save the delicious garlic-infused oil for use in other recipes.

When sautéing garlic, don't let it turn dark brown because it will taste bitter. If it starts to burn, lower the heat or remove the garlic from the pan immediately.

Mozzarella

This cheese was originally made from the milk of the water buffalo *(mozzarella di buffala)* and, while that type is still available sometimes, it is rare. This is a versatile fresh cheese and the key word is fresh. The shelf life is about a week. In Brooklyn, no Italian worth his weight will eat a mozzarella that has been refrigerated. It should ideally be made and consumed in the same day.

Olives

It can be confusing to select the correct type of olive for a particular use. There are thousands of types of olives, but the following is a list of the most common ones available in stores:

Gaeta These are imported from a small town of the same name near Naples. They have a remarkable flavor and are either brine-cured or salt-cured and rubbed with olive oil. The brine-cured are good for snacking or cooking. The salt-cured are for snacking only.

Calabrese Tiny green olives from Calabria that are traditionally brine-cured with herbs and hot pepper, in keeping with the overall spiciness of Calabrian food. These are for snacking only.

Large green Sicilian Obviously from Sicily, usually cracked before being cured in brine with vinegar. They are great for *Insalata di Olive*, olive salad.

Kalamata These Greek olives, which are cured in brine and vinegar like the Sicilian, are readily available and inexpensive. They are good substitutes for Gaeta. If you find them too vinegary, just blanch them in boiling water for 20 seconds.

Homemade cured olives

There are two ways to cure olives, with lye or with water and salt. I never use lye because the mere thought turns me off. I use the brine method, which in Italian is called *olive alla salmaria*. Start by filling a barrel with the olives. To measure the salt, fill a bucket with tap water and place a whole fresh raw egg inside. The egg will sink to the bottom. As you add the salt, the egg will begin to float. Keep adding salt until the egg bobs to the surface. Take out the egg and pour the water into the barrel. Add a few hot chiles, a few whole heads of garlic, and a few tops of fennel bulbs. There is no exact amount of each ingredient to use, just add them to your taste. After 4 months, change the water. Drain the old water, leave the seasoning and repeat with fresh water and salt. Let the olives cure for another month, drain the barrel again, and repeat the process one more time. After 6 months, drain the olives, but this time cover them with lightly salted water, leaving the seasoning. You can now pack them in jars and they will last as long as 2 years.

Olive oil

This is one of the most important ingredients in our Little Italy cuisine. Many of the recipes in this book call for "extra virgin olive oil," which is the purest, tastiest form. Extra virgin has no more than 1% acid content, it is a beautiful dark green color, and it has the most olive oil flavor. To make it, the olives are cold-pressed, a simple process with no chemicals or refining. Virgin olive oil is a grade below extra virgin; it has slightly more acid (1 to 3%). Anything that is labeled simply "olive oil" will be a lesser grade, often a blend of olive oils, which are refined and processed. There is also a product called "light olive oil," which is somewhat misleading. It's not actually lighter in calories; it's simply been refined to be lighter in flavor and color.

In general, extra virgin olive oil can be used in any instance when olive oil is called for. You especially want to use it in recipes where it's uncooked, such as salad dressings and garnishes. For cooking, you might want to use a lesser grade, since extra virgin can be expensive. You sacrifice some flavor but you save some money. The only time it's recommended to use a lighter, refined oil is when you are cooking at high temperatures, for instance deep frying, since the lighter oils have a higher smoke point.

Parmesan Cheese

When it comes to grated cheese as a garnish for pastas, soups, and other Italian dishes, there is nothing to match freshly grated Parmesan cheese. It is made from skimmed or partially skimmed cow's milk. In order to qualify as official "Parmegiano-Reggiano," it must come from the region around the city of Parma in North Central Italy and be aged at least 2 years. It has a moist but very firm and grainy texture, which makes it perfect for grating. It is relatively low in fat and high in protein. *Grana Padano*, which is made outside the key region to slightly less stringent standards, is an acceptable substitute for genuine Parmesan. Pre-grated, imitation, or processed versions are not.

Pasta

First, it is important to use a large enough pot and enough water for the amount of pasta you are cooking. The rule of thumb is to use 5 quarts of generously salted water per pound of pasta, and to cook over high heat. Second, stir continuously so the pasta doesn't stick to the pot. Don't cover the pot; it'll boil over and make a mess. Leave the pasta al dente, and don't over-sauce it. Depending on the thickness of the particular cut of pasta you're using, you should cook it for 12 to 16 minutes. Most packages have instructions. Always remember, too, that if you leave pasta in a hot pot on a hot stove, it will continue to cook even after you turn off the heat. Take care not to overcook pasta because it can become starchy, mealy, and mushy. In the case of fresh pasta, you should just drop it in boiling water for 2 to 3 minutes. And be extra careful, because fresh pasta is very easy to overcook.

A word about pasta dishes as a first course or a main course. Traditionally, in Italy and in the Italian-American culture, pasta is the first course of a multicourse meal following the appetizer or antipasto (literally, "before the meal") and followed by the main course of meat, fish, or chicken. In the past 10 or 15 years, pasta has become very chic. It's considered fashionable and healthy to serve pasta as the main course either for lunch or dinner accompanied by an appetizer, salad, or vegetable side dish. Most of the pasta recipes you'll find in this book were intended as first courses in a multicourse feast, but could also be served as a main course. One pound of pasta will yield generous portions for four people. If you want to serve a light lunch or the first course for a hearty dinner, just divide that pound of pasta into smaller portions for six to eight people.

Nowadays you see a lot of fresh pasta, even in delis and supermarkets, not just in the specialty stores. Pasta, however, is one case where fresh is not always best. The fresh pasta is heavier than dried because it's closer to a dough. And frankly, many of the companies that make fresh pasta just don't do it all that well. On those special occasions when you decide you want fresh pasta, make it at home. Take care to cook it properly—a very short time—and if you have to store it, either freeze it (for up to a month) or refrigerate it in an airtight container (no more than about 3 days).

There are many brands of well-made dry or "factory" pasta widely available. The quality is consistent and there are many, many shapes.

Here are the basic types of pasta and some examples of the most familiar shapes:

Short These are good as additions to soups or stews or in casseroles; some examples are ditali or ditalini (small, pinkie-size tubes), shells, rotelle (wheels), rotini (small spirals), pastina.

Medium These are good for thick, chunky *ragu*-type sauces or a heavier cream sauce: rigatoni (tubes with ridges), penne (tubes cut on the bias), farfalle (butterflies), orecchiette (little ears), fusilli (spirals).

Wide Paparadelle are the classic extra-wide noodles that go very well with a hearty *cacciatore* (hunter's) *ragu*. Lasagna, which are prepared in the classic baked dish, are another type of wide noodle; along with manicotti and cannelloni, they are the only ones that are precooked.

Long These include spaghetti, vermicelli ("little worms"; very thin spaghetti), capellini (angel hair), perciatelli (like spaghetti but hollow and thicker), bucatini (like spaghetti but hollow), fettucini (long noodles). They are best with lighter, thinner sauces such as clam sauce—they grip the sauce when twirled on your fork. Vermicelli, by the way, work well broken in half for soups.

Filled Tortellini (twisted, doughnut-shaped), tortelloni (large tortellini), agnolotti (crescent-shaped ravioli) and ravioli come pre-filled, whereas cannelloni and manicotti, both large, long tube shapes, must be filled in your kitchen.

Roasting peppers

The end-of-the-summer pepper-roasting is a ritual with my grandmother. She spends 3 to 4 days roasting peppers and jarring them for the winter.

The easiest way is to wash the peppers and place them directly on the gas burner, or under the broiler, turning them continuously until they are completely charred. Then place them in a paper bag for 15 minutes to steam. Remove from the bag, peel, and remove the stem and seeds. At this point, you can place them in a jar with a few garlic cloves and basil leaves, cover with olive oil, sterilize, and store for the winter.

Scallops

When buying scallops, check to make sure that there is no smell at all except for a fresh aroma of the sea. Also, always insist that they are "dry." Irreputable fishmongers will soak scallops in liquid. The scallops will act like a sponge, soaking up the liquid, and the consumer ends up paying for added weight. Soaked scallops don't cook well

because the trapped water flows out into the pan causing them to steam instead of sauté. Although there are hundreds of different species of scallops in existence, the only three that you will commonly find at your local market are:

Sea scallops They are the largest, ranging in size from the diameter of a quarter to that of a half dollar. They are harvested all year round so you shouldn't have a problem getting them fresh.

Bay scallops Atlantic Bay scallops are the most delicious and succulent of all. They are also the least plentiful since they are not available in the summer.

Calicos They are very small. It takes 150 to 200 to make a pound. They are often sold as bay scallops, but they aren't as flavorful as the real thing. They are also the least expensive.

Sugar

To jazz up your ordinary sugar for use in baking or for your favorite iced tea recipe, take vanilla pods, from which the beans have already been removed, place them in an airtight jar with granulated sugar and allow to stand for at least 2 weeks in your pantry. Remove the pods from the sugar, chop them fine, and sprinkle them on your favorite dessert plate. It makes a beautiful decoration and creates a great aroma.

Conversions

Weight equivalents

The metric weights given in this chart are not exact equivalents, but have been rounded up or down slightly to make measuring easier.

Avoirdupois	Metric
¼ oz	7 g
½ oz	15 g
1 oz	30 g
2 oz	60 g
3 oz	90 g
4 oz	115 g
5 oz	150 g
6 oz	175 g
7 oz	200 g
8 oz (½ lb)	225 g
9 oz	250 g
10 oz	300 g
11 oz	325 g
12 oz	350 g
13 oz	375 g
14 oz	400 g
15 oz	425 g
16 oz (1 lb)	450 g
1 lb 2 oz	500 g
1½ lb	750 g
2 lb	900 g
2¼ lb	1 kg
3 lb	1.4 kg
4 lb	1.8 kg
4½ lb	2 kg

Volume equivalents

These are not exact equivalents for the American cups and spoons, but have been rounded up or down slightly to make measuring easier.

American	Metric	Imperial
¼ t	1.25 ml	
½ t	2.5 ml	
1 t	5 ml	
½ T (1½ t)	7.5 ml	
1 T (3 t)	15 ml	
¼ cup (4 T)	60 ml	2 fl oz
⅓ cup (5 T)	75 ml	2½ fl oz
½ cup (8 T)	125 ml	4 fl oz
⅔ cup (10 T)	150 ml	5 fl oz (¼ pint)
¾ cup (12 T)	175 ml	6 fl oz (⅓ pint)
1 cup (16 T)	250 ml	8 fl oz
1¼ cups	300 ml	10 fl oz (½ pint)
1½ cups	350 ml	12 fl oz
1 pint (2 cups)	500 ml	16 fl oz
2½ cups	625 ml	20 fl oz (1 pint)
1 quart (4 cups)	1 litre	1¾ pints

Oven Temperature equivalents

Oven	°F.	°C.	Gas Mark
very cool	250–275	130–140	½–1
cool	300	150	2
warm	325	170	3
moderate	350	180	4
moderately hot	375	190	5
	400	200	6
hot	425	220	7
very hot	450	230	8
	475	250	9

Acknowledgments

Let me start by thanking my grandmother, Mary Lazzarino; my wife, Geri, for putting up with me; my two sons, Anthony and Paul, the greatest kids anyone could hope for; and my whole family, including Annette and Sandy.

Very special thanks to my agent Roger Vergnes of Copperplate Press, who has stood by me through this whole project; David Gibbons, who spent hours refining my English and making all this readable; Melanie Acevedo for great pictures; Leslie Stoker, my publisher, for having confidence in me; her assistant, Christina Sheldon; production director Hope Koturo; designer Alexandra Maldonado; and everyone at Artisan. I'm also grateful to Julie Stillman, Isabelle Vita, and Cathy Dorsey for additional editorial assistance.

Many thanks to everyone who participated in this project, including John, Sr., Joseph R., and the entire Profaci family of Colavita USA; Howard Bernstein of Premier Wines; Joe Generoso, Alfredo, Frank and the staff and family of Royal Crown Bakery; Sal Alba, Luigi DiRosa, and everyone at Alba Pastry Shop; Louise and Joel Ciminieri of Totonno's Pizzeria; Marc Bussio of Salumeria Biellese for the great pork products and good friendship; Iano La Verghetta and his wife, Carmela, for their hospitality; everybody at Global Tropical Fruit company in Brooklyn for their wonderful fruits and vegetables.

A warm, heartfelt thanks to Jeanne Wilensky—my publicist, confidante, advisor, and a very special lady. I wouldn't be where I am today without Jeanne. Thanks to all the staff at Le Chantilly who helped me create this book by going on photo shoots, testing recipes, putting up with my moods and supporting me in general—among them Thomas Harris, Carlos Olivar, James Fox, Peter Mayers, and Mayra Del Valle, the master recipe taster.

The most special thanks of all to my mother, Constance Lazzarino, who loved and protected me.

Mail-Order Sources

Alba's Pastry Shop
7001 18th Avenue
Brooklyn, NY 11204
(718) 232-2122
Marzipan, cheesecakes, pastries

Colavita USA
P.O. Box 9143
Elizabeth, NJ 07202
(800) 665-4731
Olive oil, vinegars, and other imported Italian products

Salumeria Biellese
376-378 Eighth Avenue
New York, NY 10001
(212) 736-7376
Prosciutto, salami, sausages, and other pork products

Index

Designed by Alexandra Maldonado

TYPEFACES IN THIS BOOK ARE BAUER BODONI, CAFE MIMI AND DELECTABLES

PRINTED AND BOUND BY ARTE GRAFICA, S.P.A

VERONA, ITALY